HOW TO BE A PHILOSOPHER

Hugh Hunter

How to be a Philosopher

Hugh Hunter

Copyright © 2020 by Hugh Hunter

ISBN 978-1-7773541-0-7

Hugh Hunter
jhughhunter.com
2020

For C., with love

Table of Contents

INTRODUCTION

WHY

Teaching philosophy can be wonderful, for you are introducing your students to thoughts that will last them a lifetime. But as my years of university teaching drew to a close, I felt a growing sense of embarrassment at the state of the academic discipline to which I was introducing my students. Many of their other teachers were not particularly interested in philosophy, and were really there to talk about some bundle of foolish activist causes. Many other academics were tired of the game of trying to find new takes on philosophical ideas that had already been picked over for centuries. They were exhausted, cynical, writing things they didn't believe and counting down the days to retirement.

If I was falling out of love with professional philosophy, the feeling was mutual. I had graduated from a top-tier university with publications already under my belt. But like so many of my peers, I did not find a full-time professorship. And as the years passed, and I made teaching into a kind of hobby on the side of my full time work, I began to encounter talented young people outside the university who looked in at the study of philosophy with a certain amount of envy and longing. They were wise enough not to imagine that the study of philosophy would help their careers, much more sensible and practical than my students or than I had been at their age. But they had a wistfulness about what it might have been like to be a philosopher.

I realized that these young people had been tricked into believing that the only way to really be a philosopher is to be a *professional* philosopher. I tried to explain to these academic outsiders that ideologues and burnouts at the university aren't philosophers. And that many real philosophers are outsiders who have nothing to do with the university.

WHAT

Then, some years ago I re-evaluated the amount of effort I was pouring into my teaching hobby. I realized I no longer found it worthwhile. It was finally time to practice what I had preached and find out whether I too could be a philosopher outside of the academy. Leaving a place where I had occupied a clearly defined role, first as student and then as professor, helped me to clarify the two motivating impulses of this book.

First, I became aware of how much I had been relying on the university. I felt the absence of what I had taken for granted for much of my life: a steady stream of intelligent interlocutors and well-rounded speakers, as well as a mighty river of research, always washing up new stimuli for my own work. At first I missed it tremendously, and only pride kept me from going back and accepting another teaching contract. But after the initial sense of loss had worn off, I slowly realized that I could enjoy many of the advantages of the university but now on my own terms, regarding the university as a public resource to be used without the need to contribute anything but my taxes. It is not an approach that the university invites, but it was not hard to do. Explaining how to do this is one of my reasons for writing.

My second reason is more wide-ranging, so let me take a few steps back to set it up. The university isn't just in a contraction or in a slump. It's slowly dying; a big beast weighed down by the same egalitarian ideologies and parasitic managerial elite gnawing away at public life across the West.

Although the university is dying, this is not its first time on its deathbed. The university gave itself over to pointless, sterile scholarship four centuries ago. The period that we call 'early modern', roughly 1600 – 1800, was dominated by a revolt among philosophers who left the university behind. The university still existed, as it does today. Professors of philosophy there still studied something or other. Few scholars today could tell you what, for we have forgotten the names of the people who stayed. Philosophy flourished outside the university. It lived in social clubs and salons, out among ordinary people.

As the university dies, philosophy emerges elsewhere. This is an occasion for hope. Let the university question the legitimacy, indeed, the morality of reading the works of great white men. Let the institution toil away on pointless distinctions and ridiculous scholarly projects of no interest to the outside world. The great canon of Western thought is on offer free to anyone who will have it. Those of us beyond the shadow of the ivory tower could ask for no greater inheritance, no richer gift.

HOW

So how do you stretch out your hand and accept the gift of philosophy? In the chapters that follow, I will offer an answer.

In the first chapter, I ask the question, "Who is the philosopher?" The philosopher, I argue, is nothing more than one who is a friend of wisdom. Just as there are varieties of friendship, so there are also varieties of philosophers.

In the second chapter, I present two sorts of tool for navigating the lands of wisdom: what I call a map and what I call a compass. I offer three maps, any of which can be used for navigation. The compass is a way of orienting yourself on philosophical questions.

The third chapter turns from the subject of philosophy to the art itself. I show how philosophy can be thought of as conceptual product-testing. The skills of a philosopher run deeper than the memorization of logical forms. They are rather the skills of the product tester who probes for weakness and failure in a machine or invention. Philosophers bring the same approach to ideas, both those of others and their own.

The fourth chapter is about the way that philosophers express themselves in language. Looking at a passage from David Hume, we find seven rules for making philosophical writing persuasive and clear.

The fifth and sixth chapters deal with more practical matters.

In the fifth chapter, I discuss forms of philosophical writing. We will see how academics write, and some alternatives. Whether you are setting out to write philosophy or to read it, this overview will help you to see where to start.

Philosophers have always needed communities. In the sixth and final chapter, I consider how philosophers should look for philosophical community. There is the university, of course. But most readers of this book won't want to make the university their primary home. Others attempt to shoehorn philosophy into their everyday lives, trying to create philosophical community at work or in their families. These approaches, too, have characteristic downsides. What has much more promise, I think, is to imitate the period of early modernity, and build philosophical groups and audiences outside the university. I will close by talking about how that might be accomplished.

This book would not exist without my family, whose help with drafts, insightful conversation and continual encouragement helped me far more than they know.

1 - WHO IS THE PHILOSOPHER?

LOOKING FOR THE PHILOSOPHER

THE BAD NEWS

I'll start with the bad news.

There has never been a worse time to study philosophy at university. It's a terrible time to study philosophy no matter whether you do an undergraduate degree or something postgraduate, an MA or a PhD.

For one thing, a degree in philosophy won't help you find a job, either in the academy as a professor or outside it as anything else. Once upon a time, degrees in philosophy were rare and therefore semi-prestigious. Those days are over.

A degree in philosophy also may not teach you much about philosophy. As a student, it would be up to you to seek out professors who are more interested in philosophy than in one of the many forms of academic activism now common in schools, professors who are not yet burned out from the requirement to constantly publish, whether they have anything to say or not. Only you would know if you were succeeding, for your grades would not reflect your success. Universities don't like to see one of their paying customers leave just because he failed a course, so courses have become much harder to fail. One of the institutions where I taught had an honest name for their students, which they only used in their corporate documents. They called students BIUs: Basic Income Units. So that's the bad news.

THE GOOD NEWS

The good news is that you do not have to study at university to be a philosopher. Socrates (469 – 399 BC) didn't. Plato (429 – 347 BC) didn't. Baruch Spinoza (1632 – 1677) didn't. Ludwig Wittgenstein (1889 – 1951) did – but only after publishing a world changing book of philosophy.

Philosophy has existed for longer outside the university than inside it. But we have become so used to thinking that the real philosophers are professional philosophers that it can be hard to visualize the philosopher in any other condition. That's what this book is about. I want to show you who the philosopher is, and how to think, read, write and seek community as a philosopher does. So let's get started.

Who, then, is the philosopher?

THE UNWORLDLY PHILOSOPHER

One view that has been popular since ancient times is that a philosopher is a particularly unworldly person, a dreamer detached from practical and immediate things. Thales of Miletus (6th century BC) was reputedly on a night walk outside, busily contemplating the stars. He didn't look where he was going and fell into a well. The servants laughed and made fun of him as they hauled him out. Everyone saw the irony. Thales the philosopher was an impractical man, whose drive to understand the most important things made him ignore what was right under his feet.

Like most stereotypes, the one about the unworldly philosopher contains an insight about the world. Philosophy is not a practical art. Many philosophers do lose interest in practical questions. Unlike a warrior or an artist, a philosopher does not produce something that can be easily identified.

I don't know whether it was the incident with the well, but Thales in particular seems to have resented this characterization of the philosopher. Like many of the early Greek philosophers whom we call the pre-Socratics, Thales was interested in the stars and the natural world, and was likely the beneficiary of a repository of Babylonian astronomical and astrological wisdom. When people told Thales that philosophy got you nowhere, he took advantage of his knowledge of seasonal change and made a shrewd guess that the next year would be a big year for olives. Thales paid in advance to have the use of all the presses that made oil. When the big crop came in, he got rich by selling access to the presses which he had reserved.

Thales wasn't just showing that looking at the stars could have practical implications. He was also combining philosophy and economics in a new way. Indeed, he may have invented the "call option," paying now for the right to buy something at a fixed price in the future. His point was that philosophical thinking can be applied to non-philosophical problems, with considerable success. The philosopher *can* be practical. It's just that he doesn't often want to.

We philosophers remember our own for their impractical, unworldly ideas, but many philosophers weren't unworldly people. René Descartes (1596 – 1650) may be famous for locking himself in a room in an inn and conducting a total inventory and examination of his beliefs, as documented in his *Discourse on Method*. But he was also a rover and a gentleman mercenary who served across Europe. On one occasion, Descartes was on a ship, and he heard the sailors plotting to kill and rob him, speaking in a language they did not think he would understand.

Descartes' solution was elegant. He walked out onto the deck, drew his sword and told them in the same language to come at him. They were so intimidated that the philosopher made it to shore.

Another philosopher, Diogenes of Sinope, also known as Diogenes the Cynic (412[?] – 323 BC) was not so lucky on his own sea voyage. He was captured by pirates and then, as was the brutal custom in the ancient world, sold as a slave. Slaves would ordinarily declare their skills, since a skilled slave was less likely to be purchased for use in a mine or in some other back-breaking work. Diogenes, oddly enough, said that his skill was 'ruling'. But one of the men in the audience thought he understood what Diogenes meant. He hired the old philosopher as a tutor for his sons, to *rule* them, so to speak. The crusty old philosopher soon became a cherished member of the household.

Philosophers have been entrusted with the most important and delicate of tasks a society has to offer. Both Gottfried Wilhelm Leibniz (1646 – 1716) and David Hume (1711 – 1776) were diplomats. Willard van Orman Quine (1908 – 2000) worked as an intelligence officer. I think it is fair to say that the philosopher has an interest in impractical matters, but it does not follow that the philosopher is himself an impractical person. So we have not yet arrived at a definition of the philosopher.

THE PROFESSIONAL PHILOSOPHER

Who, then, counts as a philosopher? It's easy to think that only a professor of philosophy is really a philosopher. It's true that if you are paid to do a thing, it suggests that your customers must believe that you do it well. And indeed, I think that many university professors are philosophers. But the question is not whether some professors are philosophers but whether *only* a paid philosopher can be a philosopher.

To calibrate our thinking, let's try an analogy. Would we say that only a paid artist is an artist? Or that only a paid warrior is a warrior? In both the case of the artist and the warrior, being paid to do a job is a pretty good indication that you are doing it competently. This is true even though some soldiers run from battle and some artists are clever grifters. But for both the warrior and the artist, the payment is only an *indicator.* Plenty of citizen warriors or guerilla fighters don't get paid. Plenty of artists aren't recognized until after they have died. Their accomplishments show them to have been warriors and artists, regardless of whether or not they were professionals.

So, we must ask, were there great philosophers who were not professional philosophers? And the answer is yes, there were many of them. Socrates wasn't a professional: he had a day job as a craftsman. St. Augustine of Hippo (354 – 430 AD) was a teacher, but he gave up in disgust and became a bishop. Gottfried Wilhelm Leibniz (1646 – 1716) earned his money as a librarian. David Hume (1711 – 1776) achieved financial independence as a writer of history. These men are among the greatest philosophers who ever lived. Clearly, one does not need to be paid to be a philosopher in order to be one.

THE PRODUCTIVE PHILOSOPHER

Did we perhaps go wrong by stating above that philosophy is not a practical art? After all, we recognize many great philosophers by their works, just as we do great warriors and great artists. A warrior produces strategies, tactics and, in the end, victory. An artist produces beautiful objects that illuminate our understanding of the world. Doesn't a philosopher have a characteristic product?

It's tempting to say that a philosopher is one who writes books about philosophy. And it is true, many philosophers have produced books. But that can't be the product we are looking for. Socrates never wrote anything, and yet he is arguably the greatest philosopher who ever lived. The Sceptic Carneades (214 – 129/8 BC) rejected all belief, and so would have found it pointless to leave anything in writing. And yet his way of organizing his contemporaries by their understanding of the *telos*, the goal of life, a model Carneades invented to make it easier to refute them, has completely shaped our understanding of his period. J. L. Austin (1911 – 1960), perhaps the greatest of the ordinary language philosophers, left no writings of his own. His books were produced from student notes.

We might say that philosophers leave a legacy through other means, as Carneades and Austin did. But even that does not seem correct. The great philosophers of history were engaged, in their time, with philosophers who left little or no legacy. Today we can barely remember Diagoras the Atheist (5th century BC) or Richard Burthogge (1638 – 1698). But these were interlocutors of others whom we recognize as great philosophers. And while history has not offered them a place in the canon, they were still men of talent, respected by philosophers whose respect was not easily earned. Most of us would be lucky to accomplish as much as they did.

The philosopher, then, is not necessarily a dreamer, or a professor, or an author, or even someone whom history remembers. Who is he?

Friends of Wisdom

Philo-Sophia

When we go looking for the philosopher, it's easy to overlook a clue which is right there in the word 'philosophy'. The word is sometimes attributed to

Plato, but in fact it is older and goes back to the semi-mythical philosopher Pythagoras (570 – 490 BC, if he existed). The word comes from the Greek, *philosophia*, a union of the words *philia*, which means love, and *sophia*, which means wisdom. We find these roots in other words today. Philadelphia is the city of the *philia* among brothers (*adelphoi*): the city of brotherly love. Sophie is a girl's name meaning 'wise'.

There's an ambiguity in the Greek word *philia* that is hard to capture in English. The English word love is often used to indicate an overwhelming, usually romantic passion. But a different Greek word, *eros*, from which we get the term 'erotic', refers specifically to overpowering romantic love. *Philia* usually refers to a love that is less overwhelming but also more stable, something lasting. That's why one of the translations for *philia* is friendship.

Philosophy, then, shouldn't be translated as love of wisdom. Philosophy is friendship with wisdom.

If we understand philosophy as friendship with wisdom, we finally have a definition that can accommodate the history of philosophy. Friendship is flexible; there are many ways to be friends, some professional, some less so, some that demand a great deal of effort and some that don't. Unlike romantic love, friendship doesn't make demands on your whole life. Friends help each other and enjoy each other's company, but they also enjoy breaks from each other's company. That's one of the differences between friends and lovers.

Romantic love for another person is aimed at some sort of consummation: sex, marriage, the production of children. Friendships have no goal beyond themselves. Friends spend time in each other's company, and that can be accomplished in many different ways. Perhaps you go camping with one of your friends, but *my* friend and I have lunch on Fridays. No one would suggest that you or I are 'doing' friendship wrong. Both of these are ways of being friends. When it comes to friendship with wisdom, or 'doing philosophy', we should likewise acknowledge that there are many ways to get it right.

WHAT KIND OF A THING IS A FRIENDSHIP?

If we consider a friendship as a whole, something that exists in space and time, like a chair or a tree or a person, friendship has the interesting property of being gappy. There are gaps in a friendship, for it is broken up in space and time. For example, one of my friends and I have lunch every few months. The discontinuous chunks of time in which we are having lunch, plus the time we spend chatting by email and text, plus the time we think about one another in between meetings, is the body of the friendship. That's all there is to it.

A song is an entity that is spread out across time, but is not gappy. If I sing "For he's a jolly good fellow" for your birthday, I have to make sure all the parts of the song are lined up one after another. I can't start the song, eat some cake, sing a little more, and finish singing the next day. That's not how songs work. But that is how friendships work. Days and sometimes weeks go by where I do not communicate with or even think about the existence of my friends. But this doesn't threaten the integrity of the friendship, because friendships are gappy objects, made up of chunks spread across the timelines of our lives.

A friendship ends when there is no further chunk of friendship. That is to say, a friendship ends the last time two friends meet, or correspond, or think about each other. Interestingly enough, this means we are often unaware of our friendships ending. They quietly evaporate in the desert of our neglect.

Friendship with wisdom, I think, is much like any other friendship. We'll consider some variants of friendship below, but let us start by considering some of the activities that make up friendship with wisdom. You can't have lunch with wisdom, after all. If you don't engage in any of the activities that normally sustain a friendship with wisdom, if you don't read philosophy, or think about it, or write it, or discuss it, then I would say that you are not a philosopher.

DIALOGUE

First and foremost, as we will discuss in much more detail in Chapter 3, philosophy exists in dialogue. This important truth of philosophy is often forgotten. But both Plato (429 – 347 BC) and Aristotle (384 – 322 BC) maintained that the most fundamental way to do philosophy was to engage in dialectic: two (or more) people talking and trying to understand an idea.

We sometimes call dialectic 'arguing', though that word has acquired a negative sense. If angry arguing is a battle, dialectic is a war game. You may not choose or even like your starting position, but the goal is to learn from the engagement. Whether you win or lose, everyone walks away from a dialogue having gained something.

What attracted Plato and Aristotle to dialectic was its endless malleability. The only rule is that someone asks questions and someone tries to answer them. You can plod along carefully, working out a problem step by step. Or you can begin with a thought experiment, and if your position collapses, you can make an intuitive leap to a better one. Books and articles have to spell out a single point, but you can start a dialogue in one place and end up somewhere that no one expected. That is why Plato and Aristotle both wrote dialogues, although unfortunately the dialogues of Aristotle are lost to history.

The formlessness of dialogue that so attracted Plato and Aristotle isn't just a matter of usefulness. Aristotle thought dialectic was even more fundamental than logic. That's because if you question logical principles, you end up in dialogue: the free-flowing conversation where you build up evidence and try to show that something follows. In a way, dialogue is the supreme court of philosophy, the place where philosophical ideas are judged.

Dialectic need not be formal. Plato's dialogues present dialectic as something that occurs on walks or at parties. Conversations carried out over a campfire or while hiking a trail are very much in the tradition of dialectic. Even when we think through problems alone, we may slip into mental dialogue, alternately playing the role of asking questions and trying to find answers. That's dialectic too.

Written conversations on the internet also offer a kind of dialectic. However, if I've learned anything from discussing philosophy on the internet, it's to value the human contact that occurs in face to face conversation. When two people are talking, a rich language of visual cues allows us to keep our replies short and pointed. Online conversation often turns into making speeches, replies get longer and longer and soon the structure of asking and answering is lost. Since the best way to engage in dialectic is in person, we'll discuss ways of growing groups for face to face discussions in Chapter 6.

READING OTHER PHILOSOPHERS

It would be a dream, for most of us, to travel back in time and spend a few hours with Aristotle (384 – 322 BC) strolling around the grounds of his school, the Lyceum, and discussing philosophy. But Aristotle is long dead, as are the other great philosophers of history. Even living philosophers are busy people. But there is one way to encounter them intellectually, and in fact to encounter their best thoughts: their books.

A thousand years ago, an aspiring philosopher had to work hard to get his hands on a book of philosophy. Even a hundred years ago, building a philosophical library was not so easy. Today we are spoiled with options. You can read the works of the great philosophers, or read books about those philosophers. You can listen to many of these as audio books. You can take in secondary commentary on the great philosophers in podcast form.

When philosophers encounter wisdom in writing, we enter into imaginative dialogue with the ideas that we find. To do this, you treat the book as a conversation, pausing to ask yourself, "Is that true?" as you read. Even for those of us who have read many books of philosophy, reading can often be like trying to drink from a firehose: many different ideas come through all at once, and it's difficult to stay oriented. We will talk more about being oriented, what I call bringing a map and a compass to your engagement with philosophy, in the next chapter. But it really just means approaching books of philosophy as an imaginary dialogue. The author is answering, which means that you need to ask, to apply pressure to ideas that seem unconvincing. It's only by applying pressure that you will discover the architecture of the arguments that support what is being said.

One of the ways in which philosophy is unusual is that the greatest written works are often more easy (not to mention more pleasant) to read than scholarly secondary sources. Any philosopher at any level of development will learn something from one of Plato's (429 – 347 BC) dialogues. It is a mark of a great philosophical work, Hans-Georg Gadamer (1900 – 2002) observed, that it meets you in dialogue no matter how junior or how experienced you are.

WRITING PHILOSOPHY

Another way to do philosophy is to write it. Many professional philosophers today write articles or books. And there are plenty of perfectly legitimate ways of writing philosophy beyond articles and books. You can write in the form of Michel de Montaigne's (1533 – 1592) invention, the essay, a literary and philosophical style that is at its best a work of art. You can write philosophical novels, as some existentialists did. *Nausea* by Jean-Paul Sartre (1905 – 1980) and *The Stranger* by Albert Camus (1913 – 1960) are good examples of this tradition. Of course you can write dialogues, like Plato. You can even record aphorisms, as Friederich Nietzsche (1844 – 1900) did. And nowadays, you can blog and comment on blogs, as many philosophers do. We'll consider these forms of writing in more detail in Chapter 4.

When you write philosophy, you are entering into the great dialogue of philosophy in the role of someone giving an answer. It's up to you to take responsibility for setting out a permanent record of your thoughts. People who read you will have questions. Some questions can be easily answered. Some will simply show you where you are wrong. For these we should be grateful. Other questions grow out of differences of assumptions at such a deep level that the best you can do is point out where you and the questioner part ways. In both cases, it's up to you as an author to anticipate the questions your reader will have, answer what you can and gesture at what is out of scope. In other words, it's up to you to situate your work so that another friend of wisdom will feel at home in it, in the spirit of dialectic. The clearer you are in stating your position, the more you will deal with honest agreement and honest disagreement. The less clear you are, the more you will have to deal with misunderstanding.

In Chapter 5 we will also return to the question of why people write philosophy, but we can note here that there are two major reasons. One is to set down their thoughts. Putting something in writing helps to clarify what you actually believe.

The other reason to write is to elicit feedback: it's a way of opening a conversation, often with strangers. Most of us write to be read and we hope to be challenged, admired or both. But if that's your motivation, keep in mind that the form in which you write will make a big difference. Nothing prevents you from putting together some aphorisms, but the sad truth is that few people will read them, and fewer still will pause to untangle the meaning packed into them. If your goal is to get responses that feed back into your friendship with wisdom, you will need to make your writing accessible.

THINKING AND REMEMBERING

Friendships occur, as we saw, in time and space. Just as friends can 'do friendship' when they go camping, play paintball, eat lunch, go to work or any number of other things, so you can 'do philosophy' by talking, reading or writing. But in fact friends don't really need a pretext: sometimes friends spend time together without performing any common activity. In the same way, it's a mistake to think a friendship with wisdom requires doing anything but thinking about and pursuing wisdom.

If 'doing philosophy' is your job, if you are a professor or a graduate student, it should be easy to find opportunities to think about wisdom and remember philosophical history. If you're wealthy enough or fortunate enough to control your own schedule, you might find this easy as well. But for most of us, doing philosophy takes effort because it does not fit naturally into the day. Most of us have jobs that can be mentally tiring even when not stimulating, and it is only when they are done for the day that we have time to think about what we would like to be thinking about. When you're working, your mind is on other things. When you're home, you're so tired that it's easier to watch or read something that is not so challenging as philosophy.

One respect in which minds are like bodies is that both begin the day relatively energized and run through their energy as they day wears on. Psychologists tells us that repeated decision making leads to 'decision fatigue'. For every decision that you make, the next one is a little harder. When it is time to go home, you are sick of making decisions. That is one of the reasons that it's so easy after a long day to settle on compromise food that no one really wants to eat: let's just order a pizza. If you can't decide on food, you'll probably be too tired to orient yourself in a book of philosophy, always asking yourself whether an argument has arrived at truth or not.

Fortunately, those of us who do not have the career of the professional philosopher also don't need to have his schedule. Michel de Montaigne was not a professional philosopher. He had the unenviable task of being a mayor in a time when the strife between Protestants and Catholics was tearing apart what would emerge as the French nation. Montaigne gives us a clue as to how he fit philosophy into his busy schedule. He thought of his own mind as being like a small shop, with a display room out front for those with whom he had dealings, business or personal, and a small *arrière-boutique* (or 'room behind the shop') which he had all to himself. We sometimes get so used to being out in the display room that we forget about the quiet room at the back. One way to be a philosopher, though, is to step back into the quiet of the room behind the shop.

It is from the comfort of this room behind the shop that even the most uninteresting environment can yield philosophical insights. For example, those of us who work in corporate or bureaucratic environments will be familiar with situations where process is more important than product. We plod along, checking all the boxes, getting all the right levels of approval, and then scratch our collective heads about why nothing works.

One day I was privately deploring the way we think about process and it occurred to me that it could serve as a model of perception. Many philosophers are attracted to faculty psychology, the notion that the mind is made up of different modules. These modules are sometimes explained as being like processes in a machine, each one initiating the next stage of the process. Your senses pick up a signal, your imagination puts it together, your understanding processes it, your judgment evaluates it, your will approves of the judgement, and a response is initiated. It occurred to me that this model of the mind functions like a bureaucracy. A stimulus arrives in the mail room, or nowadays, in the digital mailroom of email, created and maintained through the efforts of the IT department. Some student or intern formats it for analysis. Some analyst understands it, summarizing the situation in a memo or report. Middle management forms a judgment about the situation, checking the memo and identifying options. Senior management, like the will, reads the summary and provides or denies approval, and then the machine of bureaucracy lurches in one direction or another.

Those who defend faculty psychology often use it as an argument against free will. That's because each stage seems to determine the next stage. The senses can only sense what's in front of them, the imagination can only act on what has been sensed, the understanding can only consider what the imagination serves up, the judgment is just picking the most reasonable option from what the understanding has offered, and by the time things get to the will, it is just a matter of rubber stamping the best course of action that the judgment has already identified. There's no room for freedom in that process.

I am one of those philosophers who doubt the truth of faculty psychology. I used to say that I just don't think the mind works like a bureaucracy. But it occurred to me that my bureaucratic model of the mind is actually what we tell student interns on day one. Anyone with experience knows it doesn't really work like that. Sometimes an email goes directly to the boss and he makes the call without consulting anyone, like an act of will without judgment or even understanding. Lots of files get bogged down in the analyst or middle management stage, like sensations we don't bother to think about, even though sometimes they are important. Bureaucracy is full of cases where things happen in a way that is not captured by the official process.

Here, I now found, was a way to conceptualize freedom in terms of bureaucracy. Most of the time the executive, the will, is *able* to proceed as he likes. Listening to the analysts and middle managers helps, but the decision is independent of all that input. That's why the executive, like the will, can shoot from the hip and make decisions based on gut instinct or intuition or on nothing at all. It's not doing so that makes the will free in those cases. But it is those cases that show that the will was free all along.

Drawing these connections, finding these little insights, is doing philosophy. The insight doesn't need to be written down or communicated to another person. It is more like a private conversation with wisdom, one that can be had in the mental room behind the shop. This is a part of the philosophical life that Montaigne had in mind.

Now it is true that these private conversations with wisdom will be richer if they are informed by some philosophical knowledge. In my example above, I needed to know about faculty psychology to connect it to bureaucracy. The way to refill your reserves of philosophical ideas is to remember the past of philosophy.

When it comes to filling your philosophical reserves, you don't need to limit yourself to what philosophers have written recently. The strange and wonderful fact about philosophy is that it has a living history. The ideas that are prominent today are trends, like fashions in dress. But this does not mean that these ideas have triumphed and are the only ones that can respectably be defended. On the contrary, there are still defenders of the philosophies of Plato (429 – 347 BC), Aristotle (384 – 322 BC), the Stoics and the Epicureans (both movements ran roughly from the fourth century BC to the second century AD), St. Augustine (354 – 430), St. Thomas Aquinas (1225 – 1274), René Descartes (1596 – 1650), Baruch Spinoza (1632 – 1677), George Berkeley (1685 – 1753), David Hume (1711 – 1776), Immanuel Kant (1724 – 1804), Arthur Schopenhauer (1788 – 1860), Georg Wilhelm Friederich Hegel (1770 – 1831), to name just those who immediately come to mind. This is far from an exhaustive list, and if I were to add respectable philosophers from the last century and a half it would be much longer. But the point is that philosophical respectability is a wide measure indeed. You can't respectably defend the astronomy of Claudius Ptolemy (100 – 170 AD). But you can defend the philosophies of the philosophers that Ptolemy would have known.

WHAT KIND OF FRIENDSHIP?

ARISTOTLE'S THREE KINDS OF FRIENDSHIP

So far we have rejected certain views of who the philosopher is. I've argued that philosophy is friendship with wisdom, and we have considered various ways to do philosophy, to be a friend of wisdom. We've noticed that you can be a philosopher in different ways, with many different levels of commitment. These different levels of commitment are often, I think, products of different kinds of friendship.

The best analysis of friendship is that of Aristotle (384 – 322 BC). In his book about how to live a good life, called *Nicomachean Ethics*, Aristotle identified three kinds of friendship. At first glance, it's easy to mistake these as tiers of friendship, as though one is better or more profound than the others. That isn't what Aristotle meant. The three kinds of friendship are just three different ways of being a friend to someone, or in the case of wisdom, to some*thing*.

FRIENDSHIPS FOR THE SAKE OF PLEASURE

The first kind of friendship is a friendship based on pleasure. Whether you're hiking, fishing, drinking, or people-watching, it's more fun if you don't do it alone. We feel more pleasure, more joy, when we perform certain activities with friends.

These friendships, which are built around a mutually enjoyable activity, are Aristotle's first sort of friendship. Most of us have many friends of this sort, often different friends for different activities. The person whose company you would seek out for a hike is not necessarily the same person you'd want to sit with on a patio on a summer's day.

Readers of Aristotle sometimes suppose friendships for the sake of pleasure are transitory. But if we think about our own lives, we can see that it isn't necessarily so. There are some shared activities that we only enjoy for a little while, but there are also activities shared with friends that can give us pleasure for most of our lives. We're delighted to see them, again and again, because we don't tire of fishing or playing chess or whatever it is we do together.

Friendships for the sake of pleasure are not inherently transitory, but as we change, so can the things that give us pleasure. Growing up is a good example. When I was a little boy, my dearest friends and I used to play war and king of the hill in our neighborhood. This gave all of us a great deal of pleasure. But as we grew up, two things happened. First, we lost interest in games like king of the hill, but second, and more importantly, the interests which replaced those games were different for each of us. Suddenly we had less in common, and we found more pleasure in the company of other people. This is a natural part of growing up, of course. Aristotle knew that such character growth may slow down, but it does not cease once we become adults.

Philosophy can be a source of pleasure, and seeking that pleasure is one way to be a friend of wisdom. A philosopher who is a friend of wisdom for the sake of pleasure might pick and choose among the areas traditionally considered part of philosophy. He might prefer political philosophy, say, to the study of knowledge in epistemology. He might also have interests that lie beyond philosophy; perhaps he finds equal pleasure in mathematics, politics, woodworking, model ship building, or any number of other things. Being friends with wisdom for the sake of pleasure is compatible with having many other pleasures and pursuits. It is the least demanding way to be a philosopher.

WORK FRIENDS

The second sort of friend, according to Aristotle, is the work friend. This is the person whose company you enjoy in the context of work, but would not seek out otherwise. Many of us who work in corporate settings will relate to this kind of friendship, for even corporate drudgery and foolishness can make for a kind of doleful companionship. Aristotle, of course, was lucky enough to live before there was such a thing as a corporation, so this can't have been what he had in mind.

I think Aristotle may have been thinking of soldiers. Not only do soldiers work together on challenging and meaningful tasks, they must be prepared to sacrifice for one another. Aristotle's distinction can also help us to understand why soldiers often experience shocks when they return home and they and their friends are no longer united in the same dangerous work. Suddenly, some friends take on other jobs, and bonds that had once seemed unbreakable are strained under new conditions.

You don't need to be a soldier to learn that work friendships are easily lost. Get a new job, change your supplier for some product, change where you go shopping, and work friends come and go. Occasionally, someone that you know at work may become a different sort of friend. But all too often when you meet with work friends with whom you no longer have work in common, you discover that you are no longer interesting to one another. Friendships that form at work tend to stay there.

Many professional philosophers, by which I mean graduate students, professors of philosophy, or those who in some other way derive a living from being a friend of wisdom, are best understood as work friends of wisdom. Here it is probably good to reiterate that work friendships are real friendships: as we saw of soldiers, some work friends are willing to die for each other. But the fact that one encounters philosophy at work at least leaves open the question of whether one would pursue it if not for work. The suspicion always lingers that those paid to do a thing are just in it for the money. I remember telling a fellow graduate student that I found the philosopher he worked on so boring that I couldn't imagine waking up every day to work on him. I wondered what kept him at it.

"If we don't land jobs as professors," I asked, "will you keep working on your guy? I mean, are you actually interested in his philosophy?" He looked at me as though it was a stupid question. "Of course I wouldn't," he said, and laughed at the absurdity of the thought.

I suspect that many professional philosophers, like my acquaintance, regard their work friendship with wisdom as something that exists only in the context of work, something they would happily leave behind if it ceased to be profitable. But if many professional philosophers are like this, it cannot be said of all of them. Everyone is familiar with the archetype of the professor on fire for his topic, someone who comes to class excited to encounter once again the great ideas he loves. This sort of professor may indeed be an example of our third type of friend.

SOUL FRIENDS

The first two types on Aristotle's list of friends cover friends who make us happy and friends who make work a more enjoyable experience. To understand the last group of friends, it helps to reflect on one puzzle that Aristotle was trying to solve when he was writing the *Nicomachean Ethics*.

Aristotle based his ethical theory on the insight that actions are selfish: when we pursue the Good, we are always also pursuing what is good for us. What puzzled Aristotle is that friends will sometimes sacrifice and die for each other – and not only hot in the pursuit of a common goal, as might happen on the battlefield. There is a sort of friendship, Aristotle recognized, which dissolves selfishness. Give either of these sorts of friends money or goods, and the other will rejoice as if he had received the gift. Because these friends are willing to live for one another, they are willing to die for one another as well. But how can this be true in a world in which our motivations begin from the self?

Aristotle thought that in such friendships, what occurred was a blurring of the boundary of the self, so that we come to see friends as second selves. Our souls, by which Aristotle means our minds, our whole living selves, are enmeshed with those of our friends. This extended self makes it possible to *selfishly* pursue the interests of another. Because the blurred self makes such friends act as though they shared a single interest and a single point of view, we might call them 'soul friends'.

Although the bonds between soul friends are strong, even they are not unbreakable. The union of self with other depends on a similarity of soul. It's not that soul friends need to have similar personalities, but they must be at a similar stage of moral development. Aristotle thought it would be impossible to see yourself in someone you thought was much worse, or much better, than you. Soul friendships require that both friends proceed at the same pace of moral growth. That is why it is possible to lose even the very deep friendships that sometimes form in one's youth. Perhaps this is also what fighting lovers mean when they complain that they no longer recognize one another. With distance, the second self becomes just another individual.

Philosophy is not friendship with a person, but with wisdom itself. Wisdom, of course, does not improve or decay. But philosophers whose friendship with wisdom is of this third sort have tied their moral development to wisdom, making the pursuit of wisdom the moral focus of their lives.

Two schools of philosophy stand out for cultivating these sorts of friendship with wisdom: the Stoics and the Epicureans. Zeno of Citium (336 – 265 BC) founded the Stoic school, named after a columned area adorned with paintings (the "stoa poikile") in Athens where Zeno's followers congregated. Meanwhile Epicurus (341 – 270 BC) founded the Epicurean school, meeting his followers in "The Garden", a self-sufficient commune on the outskirts of Athens. Both schools long outlasted their founders, finally dwindling away in the second century AD, though both have been revived many times, and there are Stoics and Epicureans today. What makes Zeno and Epicurus such good representatives of soul friendship with wisdom is that both philosophers promised that someone who lived in accordance with their teachings would lead a good life.

Stoicism and Epicureanism are both comprehensive guides to life. They have worked out philosophical positions on the best way to eat, drink, seek friends, fall in love, have sex, make money, survive misfortune, and die. Even religious devotion occurs through the lens of Stoicism and Epicureanism, and both founding philosophers had unconventional doctrines about the divine. In a way, a soul friendship with wisdom is a religious approach to philosophy. Every part of the philosopher's life is lived in community with wisdom.

One does not have to be a Stoic or an Epicurean to take this approach to wisdom. But it is no small thing to live one's life by the austere standard of wisdom. Wisdom offers insight and understanding, but not forgiveness or redemption. To be a soul friend of wisdom, then, requires great confidence in one's own strength and will. The very high bar is set by Socrates, who preferred execution to a life without philosophy, and met his death with the quiet assurance that "a good man cannot be harmed by a bad either in life or in death, and his affairs are not neglected by the gods." (Plato, *Apology* 41d).

ARE THERE FALSE FRIENDS OF WISDOM?

IS ONE KIND OF FRIENDSHIP SUPERIOR?

Is one kind of friendship superior to the rest? Aristotle would not have said so. In his view, a normal life will involve all three sorts of friendships. They are different, appropriate to different circumstances, but not hierarchical.

I would call myself a friend for the sake of pleasure with philosophy. We who take this view tend to have a live-and-let-live approach to other friendships with philosophy. Not so work friends and soul friends, who tend, each in their ways, to a sort of supremacism, a sense that only one kind of philosopher is worthy of the name.

ACADEMIC SUPREMACISM

Some professors of philosophy, and many who are not academics but who have a high regard for them, secretly or not-so-secretly believe that only professional philosophers are *really* philosophers. They know that this wasn't always true in history, but they'd insist that it's true now. This is the view I'll call 'academic supremacism', in that it holds that those who encounter wisdom as a work friend are better than the rest of us – at least when it comes to being a philosopher.

The reasoning usually runs along these lines. A professor of philosophy is certified in philosophy, as a mover is in moving the contents of a house. One of the reasons we generally trust movers is that they move *for a living*. This means that they are subject to some level of oversight which will, we hope, intervene if a mover does serious damage. Even more importantly, the very fact that a mover has repeat customers speaks to the mover's competence. Academic supremacists about the study of philosophy would argue in the same way about professional philosophers. Only professors are held to account by their peers; only professors draw students. Therefore only professional philosophers are real philosophers.

Anyone acquainted with professional philosophy is likely to have smiled at the last paragraph's suggestion that professors of philosophy are held to account by their peers, and that they 'draw' anybody. Most professors are only held to the vaguest rules of polite conduct: if a professor refrains from things that are illegal and grossly unethical he can more or less expect to be left alone. (This isn't true, of course, if he tips over sacred cows, and if he is an untenured adjunct all bets are off.) Moreover, professors do not really draw students. Universities and their amenities draw students, certainly, but except at the graduate level, no student goes to school with a particular professor in mind. This means that many who are professionally successful as professors publish little that wins any favour with their colleagues and have never personally attracted a single student. But for the sake of argument, let's grant the dubious suggestion that all professors of philosophy are respected by colleagues and vindicated by the free market. Would it follow that they are the only true philosophers?

It wouldn't. The flaw in this argument is that it fails to distinguish the function that someone performs from the professionalization of that function. A mover's function is moving furniture and possessions, but the mover professionalizes that function, meaning that he takes money, files taxes, keeps up on the latest shortcuts and labour saving tricks and so on. So there are really two areas where we can ask about supremacy: the function and the professionalization of that function.

If I, untrained as I am, tried to go into business as a part-time mover, or give moving advice, I'd be far inferior to real movers. I'd take much longer than the competition, I wouldn't know how to save time or pack the truck so that nothing rattles around, and I'd need to be paid under the table. As far as the profession of moving goes, the certified really are almost always superior to the uncertified. But what about in the function itself? Well, when it comes to moving my own things, or moving them in exactly the way I want, I could do that. If I am willing to take a long time and perhaps spend more money, I might even be able to move my own possessions better than a professional mover, for example by taking delicate objects in multiple trips. That is because, unlike a professional mover, I'm not trying to solve everyone's problems, just my own.

Like the professional mover, professional philosophers have a breadth of knowledge that amateur philosophers usually do not have. It's not surprising that this is the case: if you do something for work, you need to keep up on the latest in your field, even in those areas that you find dull. This depth of knowledge makes professional philosophers good at teaching college courses, for example, where a skillful teacher will be able to link a student's question to philosophical thinking across history. Professional philosophers will bring that background knowledge, in addition to certain tricks of the trade, some of which we'll discuss in later chapters, to any particular question. Their analysis will usually be richer, but it does not follow that their analysis will be better. When it comes to a particular question, just as when it comes to moving your own furniture, anyone can offer an analysis.

Just as we do not want to have an inflated sense of the professional philosopher, we also need to recognize his value. People for whom wisdom is a work friend have a professional obligation to study areas that even they may find uninteresting, but which contribute to other knowledge. Let me give as an example one of the most useful books of philosophical history that I own. It is called *The People of Plato: A Prosopography of Plato and Other Socratics*, by Professor Debra Nails. The book is a who's who for the dialogues of Plato and his philosophical environment. Plato mentions all sorts of people who were famous in his day, and if as you're reading you wonder who these people were, Nails has got you covered. Many of us love Plato, but few of us would have the energy to write a book like this unless, like Professor Nails, we were paid to do so. This is the great value of professional philosophers. Like professional movers, they are most helpful for doing work you do not want to do yourself.

PHILOSOPHICAL SUPREMACISM

Some people are friends with wisdom for the sake of pleasure, and some for work. What about those who have soul-friendships with wisdom? Just as professional philosophers are sometimes regarded as the real philosophers, so too those who give their lives over to philosophy, as the Stoics and the Epicureans did, tend to think of themselves as the only genuine article.

In Plato's *Apology*, Socrates (469 – 399 BC) is on trial, but his defence (the English translation of the Greek *apologia*) is so aggressive that one of Socrates' students, Xenophon (430 – 354 BC), thought that Socrates had engineered his own death. Socrates tells his jury that "the unexamined life is not worth living" (Plato, *Apology* 38a5-6). This is often presented as the archetypal statement of philosophical supremacy. Since Socrates' characteristic philosophical method was the *elenchus*, an examination of other people's ideas, the suggestion is that those who do not engage in such philosophical examinations are leading meaningless or pointless lives.

The philosophical supremacist says that the best life that is available to a human being is the life of philosophical contemplation. Now there is, of course, something rhetorical about this claim. Ever since people started studying philosophy, other people have been asking them, "What are you going to do with that?" The insistence that philosophy makes for the best life, or the only good life, makes for a snappy comeback.

But when I encounter such philosophical supremacists, I can't help but recall a story about Diogenes the Cynic (412[?] – 323 BC), who was once invited to become an initiate of an Athenian mystery religion. The priests assured him that initiates alone would gain access to a paradise in the afterlife. Diogenes replied with contempt that he had no time for a paradise that would include all sorts of ordinary people who were initiates and exclude the great statesmen Agesilaus and Epaminondas (Diogenes Laertius, *Lives and Opinions of Eminent Philosophers* 6.39). A similar contempt is, I think, warranted for those who say that only the philosophical life counts as good.

Did Socrates really intend this shallow supremacism? Perhaps not. There are other ways to examine a life than with the Socratic method, after all. The temple of Apollo at Delphi famously featured the inscription "know thyself" over one of its doors. William Shakespeare's tragedy, *King Lear* is a story about a good king at the end of his life. He has successfully ruled a country, but he lacks self-knowledge. His plans depend on the love and esteem that his subjects, in particular his daughters, have for him. He does not realize that many of them do not love him but only feared the power that he gives up. As a result, his plans for a comfortable and dignified old age unravel. What self-knowledge he gains comes at the cost of his kingdom, and of the one daughter who really did love him – that is why the play is a tragedy. We might say that someone who passes through life without self knowledge is a fool. Lear's foolishness costs him everything he worked for, so that at the end of his life it is as though he had not lived. In that way, his life was not worth living. This is a much more plausible interpretation of Socrates' statement.

FRIENDSHIPS CHANGE

As Aristotle recognized, friendships change. It is possible to meet someone at work and develop a work friendship, then carry that friendship on for the sake of pleasure. Over time, two people may draw close and become soul friends, only to pull apart and have friendship come to an end. In the same way, friendship with philosophy can be many things, even over the course of a single philosopher's life.

2 - WHAT IS PHILOSOPHY ABOUT?

PHILOSOPHICAL TOURISM

EVERYONE BEGINS AS A TOURIST

My first philosophical love was one of Zeno's paradoxes of motion.

Zeno of Elea (born 490 BC) was a disciple of Parmenides of Elea (born around 515 BC), a philosopher who defended monism, the puzzling claim that there is only one thing in the universe, and we are all somehow parts of that thing. Since only one thing really exists, the changes and multiplicity of things we think we see in ordinary life must be a kind of illusion. Unsurprisingly, this was a hard sell, and to make it a little easier, Parmenides' student Zeno devised his famous paradoxes. The paradoxes are meant to shake you up, to show that your belief in a world of many changing objects is contradictory all on its own. First Zeno softens you up and then Parmenides can slip in and persuade you of his metaphysical monism.

I didn't know any of this the first time I encountered Zeno, which was after dinner. My father, a professor of philosophy, had grown tired of my badgering him for another cookie.

"Yes," he said, finally, "you may go and get another cookie, provided you can answer this question."

"OK," I said, staring hungrily at the box of cookies.

"To get the cookies, wouldn't you have to walk across the room?" Dad asked.

"Sure."

"But before that, you'd be halfway there," Dad went on.

"I guess so."

"Then you'd have halfway left to go."

"Yes."

"But before you could cross the second half, you'd have to cross half of the half, which is to say, a quarter of the way."

"Yes," I allowed, not sure where this was going.

"Now to get across the remaining quarter, wouldn't you have to go half of the quarter, which is to say an eighth of the way?"

"Yeah."

"And to get over the eighth, wouldn't you have to go one sixteenth?"

"I suppose," I allowed, suddenly suspecting where this was headed.

"Do you think you'd ever run out of halves? Would you ever get to a number so small you couldn't divide it in half?" Dad asked.

"Of course not, there's no such number," I replied. I had learned this in math.

"So you'd have to travel through an infinite number of halves. And even if they are very small bits of space and you can pass through them very quickly, there are an *infinite* number of them. Do you think you can travel through an infinite number of places?"

"I don't see how I could," I admitted.

"Then I guess it's impossible for you to go get that cookie," Dad said, with a smile.

Now this, I remember thinking, *is interesting* – much more interesting than a cookie. Later I bugged my father about the argument. He told me it was called a paradox, a case where two beliefs are brought into conflict. On the one hand I believed that everything can be divided forever, at least in principle. On the other hand, I believed that I could walk across the room to the box of cookies. Now it seemed that at most one of those beliefs could be true.

"But which is right?" I remember asking.

"That's for you to figure out," said Dad, ever the teacher.

Many years later I recognized that I had been led to one of the landmarks in philosophy. Even millennia after Zeno's death his paradoxes continue to puzzle philosophers. Paradoxes are a challenge, and philosophers have a duty to answer Zeno, or if they fail, to consider that he and Parmenides might be right. But at the time I wouldn't have known how to do that. I had arrived in philosophy the way everyone does: as a tourist.

THREE MAPS AND A COMPASS

In the last chapter, I proposed that we should think of philosophy as friendship with wisdom. But as we explore how to become a philosopher, it is helpful to think of wisdom as being like a place that we can visit, a land of ideas. In order to make sense of this place, we need to fit what we learn into an organizational framework. We need a map – or perhaps several maps. The land of ideas is a little like an old European city where so much has happened that you can use more than one map. In an old city you could perhaps explore a map of the homes of famous thinkers or tour the sites of great battles and never cover the same ground. In the same way, we will see three maps that do not look very much like one another, but each can be used to get around in the land of ideas.

If you are travelling in a foreign place, it is not enough to know where everything else is, you also need to know where *you* are. The same thing is true of the land of ideas. What you need is a compass that tells you where you are on the map. People who do not bother to locate themselves on the map experience a characteristic disorientation. This is, I think, the source of the belief that in philosophy, anything goes and every opinion counts. It would be equally true to say that you are welcome to believe that the best thing to see in Berlin is not a palace or the museum island but a very nice sandwich shop that you discovered while wandering. There is no law against believing such things, but when someone reports having this opinion we suspect that he has not seen or understood much of Berlin. Approaching philosophy with a map and plotting our own course across that map can keep us from missing what is important.

The first of our maps is a historical map, the River of History. In order to weave together the history of philosophy, we think of different periods as leading into one another, and as collectively answering questions. What's good about this map is that since it is based on the time when a philosopher lived, you can fit anyone into the map by considering the dates of his life. One downside of this map, though, is that by stringing philosophers together around themes, we generate the illusion of historical progress, as though certain philosophers were just waiting for other philosophers to come along and clear up their difficulties. That isn't how philosophy works: individual philosophers developed complete accounts, and each of them is a perspective from which the history of philosophy can be viewed. The flow of history is an artefact produced by historians, and different historians tell the story a little differently. This is our first map.

The second map has the shape of a tree, for it is the Tree of Knowledge. It's a way of organizing philosophy by how fundamental a question is. For example, consider these two questions.

Are you the same thing as your body?

What moral responsibilities do you have regarding your body?

The first question is more fundamental than the second. That is because, in order to understand your responsibilities for your body, you need to know what your body is to you. One possibility is that you are identical to your body. Another possibility is that you are a mind and your body is like a set of clothes that you could remove and still be you. Depending on what you think is true, your answer to the second question about moral responsibilities will be different. And that is because in the Tree of Knowledge, the first question is down in the roots, whereas the second question is up in the branches where ethics is to be found.

The third map is the Marketplace of Ideas. This last map presents philosophy as a place where ideas are sold and bought in the coin of new beliefs. The Marketplace of Ideas can help us understand an often neglected aspect of the philosophical life: we consider philosophical ideas not merely to understand them, but to find out if they are true and add them to our beliefs about the world.

Whether you begin with one of my three maps or with another map altogether, you will soon transform it into your own map, making notes of features that I did not mention, and perhaps finding shortcuts and even landmarks of which I am unaware.

After all three maps, I will present a tool to help you locate yourself on the map: a compass. This compass consists of a few questions you can ask yourself to become philosophically oriented on a particular topic, and thus to enter into the philosophical conversation and put some skin in the game. In closing, I will consider a couple of areas where philosophers often find it difficult to put their skins in the game, namely faith and natural science.

Map 1: The River of History

History as a River

History can seem to be a meaningless series of events. To organize these events, historians tell stories. In this they are only doing for other people's history what we all do for our own lives, thinking of the time before we moved out of our parents' house and the time after, before and after marriage, before and after children. We do this even though we know that such milestones, important as they are, do not actually make us into new people, and that many of the things that matter change, if they do, on quite a different schedule.

In the map that I call the River of History, we are going to stride across the history of philosophy in five big steps. These five segments of history don't perfectly divide the historical flow, of course. History is fractal. Whenever you look closely at a philosopher, or at his period, you find that he does not neatly fit into the story of that period. But look more closely, and you find that there is an order there, a different order, characterizing the life and times of the philosopher. Look even more closely, and this order too evaporates, but an even more complex order becomes visible. The historian's craft is to master several levels of this order.

THE PROBLEM OF CHANGE

Our map begins in Ancient Greece. The question that puzzled many ancient philosophers was a problem related to change. How is it that your body changes, completely renewing its atoms every few years, as we would say today, and yet you remain the same thing? When I think about what I mean by a body, I visualize a constant, static object, like a mountain. But the real thing is constantly changing, like a waterfall. How can something change and still be the same thing? The poet and priest Fr. Andrew Young captured the problem in verse: "Limbs, spongy brain and slogging heart, / No part remains the selfsame part; / Like streams they stay and still depart."

The problem of change is what motivates the ancient paradox of the Ship of Theseus. Suppose that Theseus sails away in a ship and stays at sea for many years. Like our own bodies, his ship slowly wears out. But Theseus is prepared for this. Whenever a part wears out, one of his assistants rows out to meet him with a replacement. So over the years the mast is replaced, the wood that makes up the side of the ship is replaced plank by plank, the rowing benches, the sail — everything. In a few years, no part of the original ship remains. Is it still the same ship? On the one hand, it seems it must be: Theseus has been using it the whole time, he never got off one ship and onto a new one. But on the other hand, how can it remain the same thing if all the parts are replaced?

The puzzle calls for an explanation of how something can change but also remain the same. And one possible answer to the puzzle is that such change is impossible. If something changes even in a single way, then by definition it can't be the same. Heraclitus of Ephesus (around the 6th century BC) considered the problem and concluded that change-with-underlying-sameness was impossible. Heraclitus is known for observing that the world is like a river, in constant flux, and stability is an illusion. Just as you cannot step into the same river twice, you can't encounter the same object twice. Meanwhile Parmenides of Elea (born around 515 BC), whom we have already encountered briefly through his student, Zeno (born 490 BC), also believed that change-with-underlying-sameness was impossible. But unlike Heraclitus, Parmenides concluded that it is change, not sameness, that is illusory. There is in reality only an unchanging state, and anything else is a mistake. If you think that view is easy to dismiss, see if you can do better than I could on Zeno's paradox of motion discussed in the previous section.

Socrates (469 – 399 BC) entered into this conversation, but he came at the problem from a different angle. Socrates' interests were in ethics. But when he asked what a virtuous man is, that naturally led to the question of what a man is, which led to the question of how something like a man could remain the same in body or mind as he grew and became virtuous. This extension of Socratic thought was developed by Socrates' student, Plato (429 – 347 BC), who found a way to combine Parmenides and Heraclitus into a single, satisfactory account. First, the part that came from Parmenides: our minds really are in contact with a precise and unchanging reality of abstract structures, the so-called Forms, about which Parmenides was right. They remain always the same. However, the physical world in which we live only reminds us of these unchanging structures. About the physical world, Heraclitus was right: this world of constant change reflects the Forms as if through distant memory, but the order and structure we seek is not really here. Theseus' real ship is changing every instant, the idea of a single thing, a single ship of Theseus, refers to the platonic Form of Ship. This world contains nothing so stable and enduring as that. Finally, Plato sought to show that Socrates was right as well. The ethical studies that Socrates had begun turn out to be precisely what is needed to gain access to Plato's metaphysical vision.

Plato's greatest student, Aristotle (384 – 322 BC), did not locate the Forms in a separate realm. He thought of forms as being within objects. Form, he thought, is the structure that expresses an object's existence but also its potential, a little bit like DNA. Without matter, the form is only an insubstantial thing, just as disembodied DNA would be nothing but information.

Without a form, matter is just a pile of stuff, just as without DNA, a body would be a pile of unrelated organic matter. The human animal is the combination of form and matter. Aristotle's account is sometimes called "hylomorphism", which just uses Greek words to spell out "matter-form-ism".

The combination of form and matter is Aristotle's solution to the problem of change. The changes we see occur within the form-matter composite, which is the location of the underlying sameness. Changes are not changes of kind because they are all equally expressions of the form. Growing from a boy into a man is an expression of my form; it is natural for me to be a boy at 10 and a man in my 30s, and so it makes sense to speak of underlying sameness. When I die, though, the composite of matter and form that was me comes apart. That's why dead things fall apart and don't regenerate themselves, the composite no longer trying to express the form and retain its structure. Aristotle recognized that just as forms provide a biological direction, they also provide moral direction. Being good means being virtuous, which is a way of fully expressing one's form. As Plato has worked to show in the case of Socrates, the moral questions are tied to deep metaphysical questions.

BECOMING LIKE GODS

As Aristotle was writing, his one-time student, the young king of Macedon who would soon become known as Alexander the Great (365 – 323 BC), was conquering the Persian Empire and the known world. Although Alexander's empire did not last, it did have the effect of spreading the Greek language far and wide, creating a culture-boom centered on Greece, and ushering in what we call the Hellenistic era. It was thanks to Alexander that, centuries later, Jesus' disciples would decide to write the New Testament in Greek. Immediately after Alexander, however, Athens became a magnet for intelligent young men who came to study in its many schools.

Philosophers at this time were less concerned with the problem of change. Instead, they looked back to Socrates' ethical questions. The Hellenistic schools can be summed up by their attitudes to the pursuit of virtue and the good life.

To the Hellenistic philosophers, the good life was not merely a life that would leave you morally irreproachable, with clean hands. The Hellenistic philosophers knew that a philosopher could end up executed, like Socrates, or enslaved like his contemporary Diogenes (around 410 – 320 BC). Some people died in horrible agony, others watched their families destroyed. Philosophers wondered if philosophy could protect you against such twists of fate. Could philosophy provide a sort of happiness that runs deeper than emotions, a peace that can't be stolen away by bad luck? If philosophy could do this, it would make you godlike, in the sense that you would be as invulnerable to misfortune as one of the pagan gods.

The goal of Hellenistic philosophy was sometimes captured in the provocative question: can the wise man be happy in the bull of Phalaris? The bull of Phalaris was a torture device. It was a large bronze statue of a bull with a hollow inner compartment large enough to accommodate a man. The victim was locked in and a fire was lit under the statue. As the man inside cooked, his screams were distorted by the bronze-work in the bull's throat so that it sounded as though a bull was bellowing. Although there was only ever one such device made, the bull of Phalaris became proverbial as a torture device in antiquity, much as the iron maiden is today. Hellenistic philosophers wanted to know whether the philosopher could somehow retain his tranquility even if his life ended in the bull, being humiliated and tortured for the amusement of others.

The best known of the Hellenistic philosophers were the Stoics, who coalesced around Zeno of Citium (336 – 265 BC). They took their name from the area under some pillars where they liked to congregate (in Greek, a stoa), and where Zeno taught. The Stoics preached a detachment from worldly interests. The man who correctly put into practice Stoic teachings would, they thought, reorient his preferences and his outlook on the world. He would be like someone who had gained a new set of interests and motivations, recognizing that virtue means alignment with and acceptance of the laws of nature and the structure of history, and that such virtue is a better, more desirable reward than any amount of pleasure or success. It's not that the Stoic master would *trade* virtue for pleasure, anymore than the grown man *trades* romance and career challenges for the toys of his childhood. The man simply outgrows his toys, he no longer desires them. From the outside, the Stoic master would appear tough and impervious to bad luck, someone so resigned to the twists of fate that he could calmly watch the failure of all his plans. But within, having made his will one with the structure of the universe, the Stoic master felt only happiness. Thus the Stoic master would be happy, even if his life ended in the bull of Phalaris. And supporting this account of virtue came a logic, a science and a theology – a complete philosophical account.

Other philosophers doubted that a Stoic master could ever exist. Some followed Epicurus (341 – 270 BC), who had a different prescription for immunity to fate. If the Stoics stood tall to take whatever bad fortune might come at them, Epicurus showed philosophers how to provide a smaller target. The point of life, he thought, was not virtue, but pleasure. Yet Epicurus was realistic about the nature of pleasure. People who chase the pleasures of wealth and luxury and debauchery find that these are mixed with much pain. Pleasure can be had most reliably through friendship, satisfying work and moderate eating and drinking. Epicureans aimed for self-sufficiency, avoiding politics and anything else that could get in the way of the enjoyment of their lives. This approach, like that of the Stoics, lent itself to a rich philosophy, including a robust theory of natural science and a striking, if unsatisfying theology.

Four particular teachings led the Epicureans to a way of constant happiness. First, they did not fear the gods, believing that the gods were not interested in us and passed no judgement upon our lives. Second, Epicureans did not fear death, for they argued that since death is the annihilation of the self, by definition there is no self left to be harmed by death. Third, they argued that such moderate pleasures as friendships and plain, healthy food are very easy to come by. Fourth and finally, pain is easy to avoid, because intense pain does not last long and so can be endured, while lingering pain is not intense and can be endured for that reason. In either case, remembered pleasures can be used to turn the mind away from present pain. Epicurus himself was not tortured to death, but he came close, dying from kidney stones. His last days were spent in apparently happy conversation with his friends, remembering the pleasures they had enjoyed together.

In the Hellenistic period, a change came over Plato's school, which transformed into what we call the Sceptical Academy (266/8 – around 90 BC). Sceptics arrived at the view that tranquility can be found in uncertainty. They looked back to Platonic dialogues and saw Socrates, not as an authoritative moral teacher, but as a seeker who never completed his search. Every time he encountered someone else's argument, Socrates produced a devastating counterargument. The end result was scepticism: the state of not being convinced by one argument more than any other. The sceptic does not have views, because he has not been persuaded one way or the other.

To understand the role of a sceptic in an inscrutably complex world, think of an analogy: our house pets. When their owner leaves, some pets wear themselves out barking or pacing the floor waiting for the owner's return. This is pointless. No matter how hard it tries, your dog or cat will never understand the complicated motivations of employment, romance, family, income, taxation and civic obligation that cause you to act as you do. The best thing for your pet would be to resign itself to not understanding and seek the tranquility that follows. The happy pet is the one that doesn't bark or pace and worry when you are gone and is simply glad when you have returned. In the same way, the sceptics found tranquility in admitting their total ignorance. The sceptics saw their mission as undermining the arguments put forward by the Stoics and the Epicureans. Faced with the bull of Phalaris, the sceptic would have tried to approach it without certainty about whether, in the end, it might be good or bad. Or at least, that is one interpretation, for sceptical doubt corrodes everything we think we know about this movement. The greatest leader of the sceptical academy was Carneades (214 – 129/8 BC), but it was said that even his successor was not sure he had ever understood what Carneades meant.

The Stoics, the Epicureans, the Sceptics and smaller schools in Athens interacted uneasily with the rising might of Rome. In 86 BC, Athens ended up on the wrong side of a rebellion, and in retaliation the Roman general Lucius Cornelius Sulla destroyed Athens, burning the schools along with the city. This permanently ended Athenian ambitions of regional dominance, but as far as philosophy was concerned, it was like blowing the seeds off a dandelion. Philosophers spread out from the embers of Athens to every corner of the Empire, forming hubs in Rome and Alexandria. Philosophy went on, and Plato's school turned away from scepticism and toward a fusion with Aristotelianism in the movement that would come to be known as Neoplatonism.

CHRISTENDOM

Philosophy flourished within the vast Roman empire. As the empire consolidated control over a vast area of land around the Mediterranean, news of its wealth and stability spread. Then, war and the ascendancy of the mighty Huns in the faraway East caused a domino effect, driving refugee populations to the borders of the empire. Rome welcomed these refugees and tried to integrate them into the empire. But the newcomers proved impossible to assimilate, and soon the erstwhile refugees turned their fury on the empire. Rome, the eternal city that had dominated Italy for as long as anyone could remember, was sacked. Rome's western holdings broke into tiny kingdoms ruled over by warlords from among the tribes Rome had welcomed. Political collapse led to cultural fragmentation. The empire had defined itself as Roman, but now it broke into many local cultures.

During this collapse, philosophers and others slowly realized that they bore the burden of preserving what they could of ancient culture. They did not look at their role as being like archivists, preserving a dead culture. Rather, they wanted to save what was valuable and true and let the rest fall away. The empire had been in the process of Christianizing. Early medieval thinkers, many of them priests or monks, set out to preserve what was valuable in ancient culture and fully reconcile it with the Christian faith. They did not know this, but the end result of their efforts would be Christendom.

St. Augustine (354 – 430 AD), a bishop in Roman Africa, was one of the last authentically Roman Neoplatonists. His ambition was to articulate the Neoplatonic philosophy in Christian terms – and provide for his late Roman flock a doctrine that would see them through the coming darkness. Later, Boethius (477 – 524 AD) worked to preserve, and translate, all that he could of classical culture, beginning the process of preservation that would characterize the middle ages. The goal was to preserve ancient learning while integrating it with Christian doctrine, achieving what is sometimes called the great synthesis of the middle ages. And it was this project of synthesis that caused philosophy to thrive within the bosom of the Church.

In the early middle ages, monasteries across Europe preserved and remembered classical wisdom. As the medieval world stabilized, these gave way to new teaching institutions called universities. Gradually, classical texts which had only been retained in a few monasteries were copied and recopied by hand and slowly spread outward again through Europe. For this reason, the subtle logician Peter Abelard (1079 – 1142) had access to fewer texts than did the great philosopher and theologian St. Thomas Aquinas (1225-1274). It is in Aquinas that the medieval project reached its goal: you will not find a clearer synthesis of faith and reason, of Christianity with the Aristotelian tradition in philosophy.

But history rolled on, and medieval philosophers began to express doubts about this synthesis. William of Ockham (1287 – 1347), for example, began to pare down the metaphysics of Aristotle. Meanwhile the world opened up as medieval Europe expanded, reconquering Spain and pushing into the Middle East in the Crusades. Classical culture was emerging from the protective cocoon of the church, being reborn, some said, which we describe with the French word for rebirth, *renaissance*. Renaissance scholars began to feel constricted by the protective embrace of the Church. They wanted to explore the classical world as it had been, worrying less and less about the synthesis of faith and reason.

THE HUBRIS OF EARLY MODERNITY

René Descartes (1596 – 1650) was deeply shaped by Renaissance ideas. Renaissance thinkers insisted on returning to the sources of classical wisdom, *ad fontes*, and from this re-engagement grew the tree of discoveries that would branch into both science and magic. Descartes studied both and produced the scientific method, beginning with the rock of his certainty of his own existence and rebuilding philosophy and science upon this firm foundation. Europe was now looking outward, finding new worlds to the West, but also in the heavens through newly invented telescopes, and at the micro-scale in the lenses of the first microscopes. A supremely confident Europe launched explorations to map and bring order to these new worlds. The period that we call Early Modernity, and that would soon proudly call itself the Enlightenment, had begun.

It is against this backdrop of hubris that the tragedy of early modern philosophy plays itself out. Philosophy by now felt that the protective embrace of the Church had turned into a stifling death-grip that needed to be broken. These were the golden years of Rationalism, the project of building up our understanding of the world from philosophical first principles, following in the footsteps of Descartes. Gottfried Wilhelm Leibniz (1646 – 1716) and Baruch Spinoza (1632 – 1677) articulated philosophies built on reason itself. Both reasoned their way to a complex architecture of ideas. In Spinoza's case, this meant a return to Parmenidean monism. For Leibniz, it meant deploying the concept of the 'monad', a kind of mental atom, to create a new synthesis of the history of philosophy, Christianity, linguistics, new science, mathematics (and specifically the calculus, which Leibniz invented), logic, and intercultural studies. Leibniz' work is so complex and so interconnected that translating and organizing it requires a breadth of knowledge which few scholars possess, and to date no scholarly edition of his complete works exists.

The rationalists aimed to understand everything. But hubris provokes the gods, and when they respond it is with the vengeance of nemesis. The confidence of the rationalists spurred the growth of a much more cautious philosophical school in the English speaking world: empiricism. While the rationalists viewed reason as an all-illuminating sun, John Locke (1632 – 1704) conceived of reason as a candle flickering in a vast, darkened house, illuminating just enough to allow us to find our way – most of the time. Locke attacked the foundations that the rationalists had imagined were so solid. Is it really true that the mind has a certain structure and is stocked with innate ideas, like a computer that runs certain programs out of the box? Or is the mind perhaps tangled, organic, sometimes getting in the way of our ability to understand the world as it is? Building on Locke, George Berkeley (1685 – 1753) wondered whether we could ever be assured of the existence of the material world that science seemed to describe. Berkeley settled on metaphysical idealism, the view that the world must exist within our minds and that there is no such thing as matter. David Hume (1711 – 1776) chipped away even at Berkeley's sparse vision, arguing that our belief in a necessary causal order is little more than habit, and that Berkeley's own arguments against an external material world apply to the existence of minds. We are left, Hume argued, with scepticism.

If philosophy had burst free of the constraints of the church at the end of the middle ages, three hundred years later it seemed weakened, depleted. Into this moment stepped the peculiar figure of Immanuel Kant (1724 – 1804). Kant was, he said, philosophically awakened by David Hume. Where Hume had seemed to undermine any hope of certainty, Kant proposed that Hume had simply been looking for certainty in the wrong place. The structure of the world was never *out there* in the world, it was always a feature of human experience. Just as a human being sees in (what we think of as full) colour while a deer sees a world without shades of red, a human being also sees the world organized temporally, causally and geometrically. Since the world that we experience is constructed by our own minds, there is no reason to doubt science or causal connection, for these are human constructs. What would the world look like if it were not being perceived by a human being? What are things in themselves really like? Kant thought that such questions are beyond the reach of philosophy and should not be asked.

THE VERY LONG SHADOW OF IMMANUEL KANT

What had gone wrong in Early Modernity? Kant tried to illustrate the problem by imagining a bird in flight. Perhaps as a dove flies out of a foggy, miasmic valley, it finds that the air becomes clearer and flying becomes easier. So the dove flies upward, and with every wingbeat, the air is purer and finer and easier to pass through. The dove looks up above the clouds and thinks, *if only I could fly until I escape the air altogether, then at last I will be able to fly free.* But of course, the dove is mistaken: flying is only possible because of the air. Without the resistance of the air, the dove would not fly, it would fall. In the same way, Kant thought, the hubris of Early Modernity had been to try to escape the confines of a human point of view, to see the world as it really is, from God's objective point of view. When reason tries to rise above the human point of view, it plummets into Humean scepticism.

It is hard to overstate Immanuel Kant's influence on the subsequent history of philosophy. Kant's argument implied that philosophy had been on the wrong track for most of its history. The fundamental mistake was metaphysics: the study of ultimate questions lying beyond physics. It is here that philosophers attempted to escape the human point of view, to find the bedrock of reason, to solve the problem of change, to understand how God fashioned the world and why, and to ground a firm foundation for the sciences. Kant succeeded in persuading generations of philosophers that science, space, time and causality itself are not properties of the world but features we human beings introduce into our experience. This meant that the kinds of questions philosophers used to ask, questions about the fundamental nature of the universe, were pointless, because they were unanswerable. The story of the next two centuries of philosophy is a story that must be told in the gloom of Kant's long shadow.

If Kant is right, what can philosophy contribute to the world? One contribution was the study of the mind. Philosophers like Arthur Schopenhauer (1788 – 1860) and Georg Wilhelm Friederich Hegel (1770 – 1831) defended different species of idealism, the view that the world is fundamentally in the mind rather than the other way around, although both were more infused with metaphysics than Kant would have liked. Schopenhauer's metaphysics was inspired by Buddhism, centered on the idea that the illusion of self was the source of conflict and suffering. Hegel's vision was grander. His idealism located us in an inevitable historical progression, stages of history following one another in necessary sequence, all leading to a cosmic awakening of the universe as a thinking thing.

Kant had argued that philosophy failed to ground itself in the bedrock of reality. But as philosophy foundered, new scientific discoveries were continually rolling in. The industrial revolution, the steam engine, the light bulb, the airplane, the automobile. Natural science had for a long time been seen as linked to philosophy, indeed it was known as 'natural philosophy'. Now this association came to seem burdensome. Just as philosophers had broken free of the smothering embrace of the Church, many natural scientists thought the time had come to break away from the tradition of arts. And many philosophers agreed and willingly took on a reduced role in the areas left untouched by science and left open by Kant's arguments, for example ethics and politics. The utilitarian ethics and liberal politics of John Stuart Mill (1806 – 1873), and the communism of Karl Marx (1818 – 1883) were developed against a comfortable belief in scientific progress. Like Hegel, Marx saw history as moving toward a goal. But Marx defined that goal through economics: at the end of history lay the revolution of workers against the bourgeoisie and the communist utopia.

With philosophy in Kantian retreat and science advancing, it was only a matter of time until the mind itself became the focus of scientific study. In the early 20th century the study of psychology split from philosophy, slowly disentangling itself from psychiatry and Sigmund Freud's (1856 – 1939) psychoanalysis. When psychologists claimed expertise about the realm of human experience, the area left to philosophy grew even smaller, but once again, many philosophers welcomed this change. Some discerned a new role for philosophy in an almost perfect reversal of Early Modernity, when philosophers had set out to provide a foundation for science. From now on, science would be the foundation, and philosophers would take on the role of clarifying and improving the discoveries of natural science. This was elevated to doctrine by the influential Vienna Circle, a loose group of philosophers and scientists meeting between 1924 and 1936 under the leadership of Moritz Schlick (1882 – 1936), influencing many of the philosophers who would go on to lead the analytic tradition.

As the twentieth century wore on, the once mighty river of philosophy receded into two tiny pools. In the English-speaking world, philosophy was dominated by a method: the analysis of language. This approach tried to bring logic to bear on the structures of language. It was not always clear what the structures of language were supposed to reveal, and philosophers jockeyed with the emerging study of linguistics, which promised a scientific approach to language. On the European continent, philosophy occupied another niche allowed by Kant: the non-psychological consideration of human experience. It was often difficult to draw the boundary between this 'continental' mode of philosophy and literature.

It is toward the end of the 20th century that little rays of sunshine began to poke through the Kantian gloom. Alasdair MacIntyre's (b. 1929) book, *After Virtue* (1981) proposed a return to Aristotle's ethics. This ethics unapologetically presupposed that philosophy has access to the bedrock of being. Neo-Thomists, that is, modern followers of St. Thomas Aquinas, began to revive medieval accounts, which turned out to be perfectly compatible with contemporary science. Philosophers in general began wondering why they had ever found Kant's arguments so persuasive, when they are in fact not very good. As the new millennium dawned, philosophers were beginning once again to explore metaphysics, though still often tentatively, and using the old languages of analysis or the continental philosophers.

Meanwhile the forward march of natural science no longer appeared so inevitable as it had a century earlier. For one thing, science fell well short of expectations. In the middle of the 20th century, the future was imagined in terms of leisure, flying cars, free energy, palatial living and space exploration. By the end of the century computers and mobile phones had progressed, but the effect was that life was anxious, crowded, frantic, and still stubbornly terrestrial. Some sciences, like psychology, were discovering serious structural flaws, and finding that many of their foundational studies could not be replicated.

And there was another problem. Many people had imagined that technological progress would lead to moral progress as well. As our power over nature grew, so would our wisdom, and perhaps even our goodness. But science proved to have a dark side. The technology that enabled mobile communication also enabled surveillance and propaganda on a previously unimaginable scale. And while it enabled repression, it seemed unable to stand up to any sort of ideology. From Soviet Russia to grievance-studies America, yesterday's uncontroversial fact became today's edgy joke and tomorrow's hate speech. Scientists, who were supposed to guide us to objectivity, seemed to line up behind power like everybody else. Do philosophers really want to follow wherever they might lead? This is a question for you and for me, for we have reached the edge of our first map.

MAP 2: THE TREE OF KNOWLEDGE

THE TREE OF KNOWLEDGE

Thinking about the history of philosophy as a river allows us to locate individual philosophers in its ebbs and currents. Another way to organize philosophy is by topic. Since one philosopher often contributed to many topics in philosophy, we may encounter the same philosopher many times when we consider philosophy this way.

Although philosophical topics can be considered in isolation, some questions are more fundamental than others. For example, the question of whether we can know anything at all is more fundamental than the question of what we can know about politics. Your answer to the former will affect your answer to the latter. When we organize philosophy by fundamental-ness, with the most fundamental questions at the bottom, less fundamental but still essential questions in the middle, and the least fundamental questions branching out from the top, we find that we have a conceptual structure in the shape of a tree. This is the Tree of Knowledge.

THE ROOTS

Like a tree, philosophy seeks to be anchored to reality, to sink roots into the bedrock of being. Certainty can only be based on the way things are and must be, which means that the most fundamental questions will concern being itself.

One way to think about this bedrock of being is through the "but why?" questions that children like to ask. Why is the grass green? Perhaps you answer that this is because of the sunlight. But why does the sunlight make grass green? Perhaps you explain the nature of photosynthesis. Why does photosynthesis operate as it does? You might point to the laws of chemistry. Why is chemistry like that and not some other way? Perhaps you wave your hands and say that chemical laws are based on laws of physics or mathematics. But why are these laws the way they are? With this question you have entered the domain of philosophy. The questions have led you downward, to the roots of the tree of knowledge.

Physics and mathematics are not going to provide answers to these questions, because these are questions about why we live in a universe where physics and mathematics operate as they do. Our word 'metaphysics' points this out, for Aristotle called the study of these questions *ta meta ta physika*, or "the things beyond physics". Metaphysics is the ultimate court, the place where other claimants to knowledge come to be judged. Even the role of mathematics and its philosophical cousin, logic, must be judged in metaphysics. Are math and logic only stories we tell about how things are? Or are they something deeper: do they reveal the bones of the universe? These are metaphysical questions.

More metaphysics would be necessary to answer the child's question about the photosynthesizing grass. Grass works the way it does, we say, because of certain chemical and biological *laws*. But when you stop to think about it, this is a strange use of the word 'law'. There is a law against tax evasion. If you break it, and if you are caught, you are punished. But no one is punished for breaking chemical laws, because they are not the sort of law you *can* break. They are regularities that never cease to apply. But if they are only regularities, we see that our 'why' question will have to take us deeper still. Regularities don't explain themselves. If you ask me why I'm going to gamble at the casino and I tell you that it's Tuesday and that I gamble every Tuesday, I have told you about a regularity. It doesn't answer your question.

Science fiction tells stories about different universes with different natural laws, and even if these stories describe imaginary places, they are not contradictory or absurd. If in a story the main character loses his hat, and then, without explanation, the hat is there in the next scene, the contradiction takes away from our enjoyment of the story. But when science fiction imagines a world where physics or chemistry or math operates differently, we don't have that reaction. It seems that we can conceive of a world where natural laws vary from the way they are here. So it seems that we are entitled to ask why they are as they are in the real world. Do natural laws, like the laws that we make, require a lawmaker? I think the answer is yes, and without such a lawmaker we will have a difficult time explaining why the laws are this way and not some other way, and for that matter, we'll have a difficult time explaining why the universe follows any laws at all.

God (with an uppercase 'G', to distinguish Him from the many gods of polytheism) is our name for such a cosmic lawmaker. It is in metaphysics that we find the three classical proofs for the existence of God. We have just skimmed over a version of the teleological argument, which argues that the order in the universe would be inexplicable without an orderer. We might also have presented the argument a little differently, and asked why there is something rather than nothing at all. The beginning of things seems to require an explanation, and specifically an explanation in terms of a cause that is free (for what could have compelled it?) and that does not itself require an explanation (for otherwise we could ask what caused the cause). Such a first cause is what we mean by God. This is a version of the cosmological argument.

Last of all, we might have considered whether God exists *necessarily*. This brings us to the ontological argument, and it is perhaps the subtlest of the three classical proofs. One way to put it is that *if* it is possible that a necessary being, i.e. God exists, then what we are saying is that in a possible universe, like a universe in a science fiction story, there is a being without which that story, and indeed any story, would be absurd or contradictory. But if you encountered such an entity in a fictional story, you would realize that our world can also be expressed in a story, a true one, and if *no* story is complete without this being, then our story also would also be incomplete without this being. Now, God is what we mean by a necessary being. Therefore, this being must be present in our world. Or to formalize this version and bring it a little closer to the way G. W. Leibniz (1646 – 1716) would have put it, God is possibly necessary, but if God is *possibly* necessary, then God is just necessary full stop, which means that God exists.

Leaving aside the question of our Creator, we seem to live in a world of stable objects. But what are we doing when we single out a chair or a flower as an object that is separate from the dirt and air that surrounds it? Platonists insist that we are discerning chair-ness or flower-ness, abstract structures that are reflected in or perhaps present in these objects. Nominalists argue, on the contrary, that objects merely resemble one another. But if that is so, how is it that even a child or an animal can easily distinguish chairs and trees and everything else? What are the structures that we seem to discern in the world?

To answer the question of what chairs and flowers are made of, we may need to get clear on what sort of building blocks the universe contains. Is there such a thing as matter, a shapeless, unformed *stuff* that other stuff is made of? Most philosophers think so. And what about creatures like us, are we made of that stuff? Are our minds made of matter, or form, or something else? Perhaps we also need to account for mental stuff. If we have minds, are they what religions tend to call 'souls', our true selves that persist after our bodies die? Or are minds and bodies somehow entangled, such that both are incomplete without the other? Materialists try to explain everything with matter. Idealists argue that this is exactly backward: everything exists within the mind, or rather minds of all living beings. Dualists think that both mind and matter will be required for any complete explanation. Our understanding of ourselves will help us to answer metaphysical questions about people. If there is an afterlife, what goes on, our bodies, our minds, both? It may also help us to make sense of the experience of free will.

THE TRUNK

When we move up from the roots to the trunk of the tree, we find questions that while not so fundamental as those of the roots, are still fundamental from the point of view of anything higher up the tree. It is here that we find questions about how human knowledge of the world works – if such knowledge can be obtained at all. This area of philosophy is called epistemology.

In the River of History we encountered the voice of the sceptic, who raises the disturbing possibility that we might be as unable to understand the complexities of the natural world as our housepets are unable to understand the complexities of human life. We know that our own minds can be almost as dim, for example when we are babies or if we grow senile in old age. If that is the lower boundary of what human beings can understand, is there an upper boundary as well? What if the philosophical answers that we seek are above that level of complexity?

It is in epistemology that an imaginary sceptic is our main adversary, for our question is whether we can know and how, and the sceptic's role is to doubt all of our claims to knowledge. Because the sceptic is imaginary, it's up to us to supply his arguments as well as our own. Arguing with the sceptic is like playing golf: you're competing against your own best efforts.

Perhaps we can defeat the sceptic by grounding our knowledge in something that is absolutely certain, and then by reasoning our way forward from there, rebuilding our knowledge brick by brick, being cautious not to let any error creep into the process. This was René Descartes' (1596 – 1650) foundationalist project, which began with the sceptical thought experiment of a very powerful demon who made it his business to deceive the philosopher about absolutely everything. Descartes realized that one matter about which he could not be deceived was his own existence. You can exist without being deceived, but you can't be deceived without existing. Next, he proved the existence of God, and from these foundations, built up the scientific method. (Today, Descartes is often accused of arguing in a circle when it comes to proving the existence of God, but my students have found, over the years, that the accusation is not so easy to substantiate as you might think.)

Maybe, though, Descartes' whole approach to knowledge is wrong. Maybe knowledge does not have a starting point. After all, when we are born, we build up knowledge belief by belief. Maybe knowledge is not like a house, but more like a group of people climbing a mountain, each one tethered to all the others. No one climber is the anchor that holds all the others in place, but all the climbers are attached to one another, and it's those connections that secure them in place.

Epistemology is not only a matter of defeating the sceptic. It also concerns the nature of knowledge. A common definition of knowledge is that it is justified true belief. So here's what it takes for you to have knowledge: (1) you believe that something is true, and (2) that thing must actually be true, and (3) you had a legitimate reason for thinking that it was true, you weren't tricked or mistaken. Philosophers have argued against this definition, both on the grounds that the bar for knowledge is set too high and that it is set too low. You might think that it is too high, because it seems that no one but God can ever know how legitimate our reasons for belief are. Or maybe the justified true belief model sets the bar too low because justification might come about by accident: for example, perhaps you check a clock on the wall which happens to have stopped with its hands on the right time. Does that count as *knowing* what time it is?

Once we are confident about the orderliness of the world and the nature of human knowledge, we can consider how it is that knowledge about it enters our minds, which is to say we can consider the puzzle of perception.

When we look at the world and see physical objects, are these physical objects directly present to our minds? You might think so. But one reason to think that they aren't is that sometimes we are subject to illusions: the heat shimmer at the end of the road looks like a puddle, the magician looks like he's sawing the lady in half. In reality, there is no puddle and the lady is in one piece. So what you saw wasn't what was really there. What is more, we sometimes have lifelike dreams in which we perceive things that don't exist at all. In all these cases, it's tempting to say that things were one way in reality, and another way *in our minds,* that what we see is a mental reconstruction of the world, a representation. But now, enter our friend the sceptic: how do you know that your representation ever reveals the world as it is? How can you be sure that there is even a world out there, behind your representation of it?

THE BRANCHES

As we move up the tree of knowledge, we come to areas which are founded both on metaphysics, the study of what is, and epistemology, the study of how we know things, but – and this is why they are like branches – independent of one another. While discussing the River of History, I mentioned that for the last two hundred years, philosophy has been conducted under the long and gloomy shadow of Immanuel Kant (1724 – 1804). For philosophers who were influenced by Kant, the roots and trunk of the tree of knowledge were mostly off limits. Philosophy survived in the branches, and that is why things written in the 1900s often seem hard to connect to deeper philosophical questions. So what are the branches of the tree of knowledge?

First of all, once we have determined what there is and how we can know it, we might ask what we should do about it, and what we should do in general. This is **ethics**. It was ethical questions, we read in Aristotle (384 – 322 BC), that primarily interested Socrates (469 – 399 BC). Socrates proposed a view on which being good means being morally healthy, moral and physical fitness running in parallel. Aristotle formalized this account, which has come to be known as virtue ethics. But perhaps we ought not to be so narrowly focused on the agent. Immanuel Kant suggested that the proper focus of ethics was on actions, and specifically whether those actions expressed one's duty. Deontology claims that only when we perform dutiful actions, when we do what we ought, will we make our actions morally consistent. Another ethical option, this one defended by John Stuart Mill (1806 – 1873), was that we ought to ask what the outcome of our actions would be. This focus on the consequences, sometimes called Consequentialism, suggests that the right action is the one that brings about the greatest benefit for the greatest number of people.

Another branch of the tree of knowledge is **politics**. If ethics asks what we ought to do as individuals, political philosophy, sometimes studied as political theory, asks what we ought to do as a group. What political project unites us? Libertarians and classical liberals argue that the nations are best understood as

2 - What is Philosophy About?

an arrangement between independent individuals, and that consequently the state's role should be limited so that we are left to pursue our own ends. Or perhaps the state's role ought to be broader, as modern liberals assert, to safeguard fairness or the rights of citizens. Although these views are common today, they are historical anomalies: for most of history it was widely accepted that nations were more like extended families, and their role was to ensure that citizens can and do live virtuous lives. And then there is that very old question of what form of government is best: monarchy, oligarchy, or democracy? For the last hundred years or so, the West has entertained a grand experiment in democracy. Evaluating it requires the student of politics to rise above the beliefs of his own time and place. As Michel de Montaigne (1533 – 1592) observed centuries ago, philosophers who live in democracies tend to assume that only democracies are just and orderly, and philosophers who live in countries with more centralized power likewise imagine that any other arrangement means barely controlled chaos.

Another area of study is **language**. For the last century or so, language has mostly been studied through the analytic method, which entails searching for the logic in our words. Language allows us to talk about things, but what are the assumptions of language itself? Indo-European languages, for example, consist of nouns modified by adjectives placed in relations to one other.

Map 2: The Tree of Knowledge | 79

The quick (adjective) brown (adjective) fox (noun) jumps (verb) over (relation) the lazy (adjective) dog (noun). Metaphysics likewise consists of objects, or 'substances' (dogs and foxes, for example) modified by attributes (like adjectives) acting or being acted upon (described by verbs) and standing in relations to one another. There is a close parallel between our language and our metaphysics. Does that tell us something about how we talk, or is it a window into how the world really is?

Another branch of philosophy is **aesthetics** – philosophy as it pertains to art and beauty. This branch of philosophy has withered in recent years, due to a lack of consensus about whether art is about beauty, another widespread assumption that has recently come into question. Certainly much of contemporary art does not aim at beauty but instead revels in what is incoherent, disgusting, and degenerate. As a consequence, the study of art has moved away from philosophical engagement with beauty and into a project of description and definition to encompass splashes of paint on a canvas, hideous modern sculptures, performance 'art', pop 'art', conceptual 'art', digital 'art' and so on and on. A few philosophers, such as Sir Roger Scruton (1944 – 2020) have maintained the study of aesthetics the old way.

In addition to these branches, there are branches of philosophy that we might call "**philosophy of __**". There is the philosophy of history, which looks for a structure in the flow of human events. There is the philosophy of science, considering such questions as whether science is like a window on the world, or more like a tool that we use to manipulate the world. There is the philosophy of literature, inquiring into the status of literary characters and structures. For almost any discipline, you can find philosophers considering its philosophical implications. These are sometimes as interesting, and as profound, as the discipline in question.

MAP 3: THE MARKETPLACE OF IDEAS

AN OLD METAPHOR REFURBISHED

Our third map is the simplest. We can think of philosophers as selling their wares in a marketplace of ideas. All philosophers, ancient as well as modern, are in this marketplace, each one advertising his own account. Some philosophers have only a few wares to sell: a new approach to Aristotle, say, or an interesting argument about causation. Other philosophers have much more detailed accounts of whole areas of philosophy. Some offer complete accounts of philosophy itself. If you visit them, they promise, you can solve all your philosophical puzzles at once. Like anyone in any market, the questions you must answer are, first, what you are trying to buy, and second, how much are you willing to spend. Let's start with the first question.

WHAT ARE YOU TRYING TO BUY?

When we shop for philosophies, we are trying to understand the world – we are trying to find solutions to all the problems of philosophy. We are aiming for what is sometimes called systematicity: a philosophy that will provide internally consistent answers to any question. A systematic philosophy covers the whole tree of knowledge: arguments up in the branches of philosophy can be linked to a consistent metaphysics in the roots. If you are wondering about free will, the system has an answer for that. If you are wondering about whether animals have consciousness, or whether democracy is the best form of government, the system will not only have an answer, but it will fit with the answer about free will.

For most of philosophical history, philosophers would have thought it obvious that a systematic view was better than a patchwork one. However, philosophers operating in the long shadow of Immanuel Kant came to reject systematicity because Kant had said the roots of philosophy, metaphysics, were off limits. In a way, of course, that's a system too, just a very unsatisfying one. Those of us who reject Kant ought to aim for systematicity.

Developing systems of philosophy is like building a house. It's a task that consists of many subtasks: plumbing, roofing, wiring and so on. And just like someone who wants to own a house, you have three options. Option one is to build it yourself. That requires a great deal of work and expertise, and there aren't many who can do everything well. Another option is to contract out some or all of the work. In this case you would hire a contractor for the roof, say, but put the flooring in yourself. Alas, even identifying honest and reliable contractors is difficult. So the simplest option is to find a single contractor who can either do it himself or who has already done the work of finding good subcontractors. This approach gets you your house ready-made. In the Marketplace of Ideas, we have the same three options. Should we try to pick up philosophical ideas and assemble a systematic view ourselves? Should we assemble some ideas, but buy others preassembled? Or should we just shell out for a complete and ready-made system of philosophy?

The first way to systematize your thinking is to do it yourself. This can seem a very appealing task, especially for younger philosophers. It's also appealing to some new housebuilders, who unfortunately face many of the same pitfalls. Assembling a systematic view requires a very long time and a lot of talent. Even if you have the time and energy, unless you are a very gifted philosopher, your account is likely to *look like* a house that you built yourself, with the philosophical equivalent of a leaky roof and crooked floors.

The second way is a hybrid approach. Here you seek contractors to help with those things you can't or don't want to do. In the marketplace of ideas, this would mean for example that you might combine Aristotle's (384 – 322 BC) ethics with the metaphysics of John Locke (1632 – 1704). The danger of the hybrid approach is, of course, that the ideas you choose may not fit together. Aristotle's ethics is founded on an idea of substance that John Locke does not share. So it will be up to you to articulate a version of Aristotle that fits with Lockean metaphysics, or a version of Locke that has Aristotelian substances in it. This is what most philosophers end up doing: we pick up ideas that strike us as plausible, and our contribution is to make sure that they work together. Perhaps we develop our own views of a few areas, as we might tile the bathroom floor, but for the most part we make use of the prefabricated ideas of the great philosophers.

The last approach is to buy something prebuilt. Today there are many philosophers who self-identify as Aristotelians, Stoics (the movement flourished roughly from the 4th century BC to the 2nd century AD) or Thomists, meaning followers of St. Thomas Aquinas (1225 – 1274). Buying everything from one philosopher means that you will end up with a view that is time-tested and virtually objection-proof. It will in most cases be better than anything you could have designed. Your own contributions will be small, but not unimportant, for it will be up to you to discover how this view would interpret the issues of the day.

The smart shopper in any marketplace buys what he needs and no more. One of the problems with the way philosophy is taught in university today is that students are encouraged to buy irresponsibly. Professors who do not really think philosophy matters tell students to take a do-it-yourself approach to philosophy. The result is that most students end up in a leaky, crooked shack. It would be better, I think, to encourage new philosophers to buy something premade – you don't need to live there forever, after all. That was my own approach, and for me, the package was René Descartes. I decided early on that he was my guy. Over the years, I found myself unable to defend aspects of Descartes' view, and my own ideas slowly shifted in a different direction. But by then I had the advantage of seeing how a systematic view ought to hang together.

HOW TO PAY FOR PHILOSOPHY

Up to now I have said nothing about one of the most important parts of the metaphor of the marketplace of ideas: money. How do you pay for things in the marketplace of ideas? The answer is that the currency of the marketplace is new and unfamiliar beliefs. That is to say, you pay by believing things you wouldn't otherwise believe. If you want to buy Aristotle's (384 –

322 BC) hylomorphic account of human beings, you'll have to believe that there is such a thing as matter and such a thing as form.

This may seem an odd way to put it, but the point extends beyond philosophy. Imagine you and I are detectives, investigating three seemingly inexplicable art heists in our city. Somehow, the thieves are pulling it off without ever being seen on camera. Because the crimes are inexplicable to us, we already know that we are missing some key piece of the explanation. This means that by the time we crack the case, we will have to believe something we do not already believe. Maybe we will discover that the thieves have hired a gymnast who can swing in along the chandeliers to avoid being spotted. Maybe we will find that the thieves have a new technology for disabling cameras. Maybe it will turn out that there is a thief working for the galleries, so it was an inside job. But we will need to believe something new, because our beliefs as they stand are incomplete. We are shopping for explanations, and we are going to need to pay with a new belief.

But notice, if we were detectives, we'd only acquire as many new beliefs as we need. Suppose I suggest that the first heist involved a gymnast swinging in on the ceiling, the second involved a new camera-disabling technology, and the third was an inside job. You'd probably be reluctant to agree, and rightly so. You would be employing the most basic rule of practical reason: the principle of parsimony, also called

Ockham's Razor. We never adopt a more complicated explanation when a simpler one will do. It's much more likely that the thieves used the same trick every time. In the same way, in the marketplace of ideas, we are thrifty when it comes to acquiring new ideas. We want to acquire as few of them as possible.

Thriftiness is a balance between extremes, between spending too much and being too cheap to spend what is needed. Philosophers in the Marketplace of Ideas aim to strike the same balance. For example, there are many ways to argue with Hegelians or Marxists, but my overall suspicion of both views is that they have acquired too many odd beliefs about the direction of history and not got much in return. They have overspent in the Marketplace of Ideas. On the other hand, many philosophers are so cautious with their money that they buy an inexpensive materialism. This requires few beliefs that are not already part of natural science: a very low cost up front. But you get what you pay for. The meagre resources of materialism make it difficult, I think, to account for free will, or the content of our thoughts, or the beginning of the universe.

A COMPASS

KNOWING WHERE YOU ARE

When navigating with a map, it is not enough to know where everything else is. You must also know where you are. The same thing is true in the land of ideas. Philosophy is easier and indeed a lot more fun when you pick a position. If you know where you are, you know what is close to you and what is far away. You know where to go looking for agreement and where to go to pick a philosophical fight. Your position doesn't need to be permanent, and it is legitimate to be moved to a new position by the force of argument. But it is very hard to feel the force of an argument until you take a position and make yourself responsible for defending it.

Whether you're trying to locate yourself or others, my compass consists of a series of questions with several options. The answers should be thought of as cardinal directions. As you grow more accustomed to the land of ideas, you'll want to take note of more subtle distinctions in direction. For example, I identify idealism as one point on the compass. But there are many kinds of idealists, all in the general direction of idealism but each with different versions of the account.

WHAT IS THE UNIVERSE MADE OF?

The universe is made of...

matter. Materialists like Thomas Hobbes (1588 – 1679) and Jaegwon Kim (1934 – 2017) would say that only material objects exist in the universe.

mind. Idealists like George Berkeley (1685-1753) get their name from the view that the universe is made of minds and the *ideas* that these minds contain.

matter and mind. Dualists think that only mind and matter together can explain the universe. Some dualists like René Descartes (1596 – 1650) think that mind and matter interact, while others like Aristotle (384 – 322 BC) maintain that mind and matter are joined together into a single substance.

GOD'S ROLE IN THE UNIVERSE

Did God make the universe?

No, the universe came to be without divine intervention. Atheists like David Hume (1711-1776) and Bertrand Russell (1872 – 1970) aim to offer a philosophical account of a world without God.

Yes, but then God ceased to have anything to do with the world. Deists like François-Marie Arouet (1694 – 1778), better known by his pen name Voltaire, offer an account of a world where God's only role is to start things off.

Yes, God's creative act is necessary for every moment of the universe's existence. Theists like St. Thomas Aquinas (1225 – 1274) and G. W. Leibniz (1646 – 1716) argue that nothing can be understood without reference to God's creative act.

IS MAN FREE?

It seems that the laws of nature operate in deterministic ways, so that given the past the future becomes inevitable. But this seems incompatible with human free will. This means that...

free will is an illusion. Determinists like Derk Pereboom (b. 1957) think that we need to live our lives without a commitment to free will.

deterministic laws don't apply to us. Metaphysical libertarians like Robert Kane (b. 1938) and Roderick Chisholm (1916 – 1999) argue that human choice is in some way free from deterministic laws.

free will and determinism are compatible. Compatibilists, sometimes also called soft determinists, argue that there is no tension between human freedom and deterministic laws, but rather that freedom is manifest within a deterministic structure. G. W. Leibniz (1646-1716) was a compatibilist.

HOW MUCH DOUBT IS APPROPRIATE?

Scepticism should be answered...

until all doubt is removed. Foundationalists like René Descartes (1596 – 1650) argue that knowledge can and must be so secure that no sceptic could doubt it.

until all reasonable doubt is removed. Philosophers like John Locke (1632 – 1704) are willing to grant that extreme scepticism is probably unanswerable. For example, if someone asked you to *prove* that the world was not created 5 minutes ago with all your memories already present, you probably couldn't do it. But who cares? That's not a reasonable doubt.

HOW DOES PERCEPTION WORK?

When we look at the world, we perceive...

the very object we are looking at. Realists like Thomas Reid (1710 – 1796) argue that we perceive the direct object of perception. To say otherwise would be to hang the 'veil of perception' between us and the world.

a mental representation of the object we are looking at. Representationalists, also called indirect realists like John Locke (1632 – 1704) argue that we perceive a mental representation of the object. Otherwise, how can we explain that sometimes, like a straight stick that looks bent in water, our representations and the world do not agree?

HOW SHOULD WE ACT?

Something is morally good if...

it exemplifies one's morally consistent duty. Deontologists like Immanuel Kant (1724 – 1804) argue that morality is a matter of acting on the right, morally consistent principles: doing your duty, whatever the outcome.

it brings about the best outcomes. Consequentialists like John Stuart Mill (1806 – 1873) argue that morality is a matter of doing what will bring about the best outcome, regardless of one's own feelings on the matter.

it is what a virtuous man would do. Virtue ethicists like Aristotle (384 – 322 BC) argue that morality begins with being a virtuous man, that is a man who has developed moral character traits. These traits will manifest differently in different situations, but always lead to the right action.

HOW SHOULD WE LIVE TOGETHER?

The most urgent aim of society is to...

bring about the virtue of its members. Communitarians like Aristotle (384 – 322 BC) thought that society had a duty to see to the moral improvement of its members.

ensure that everyone is treated fairly. Liberals like John Rawls (1921 – 2002) argued that only a society that was fair to all could claim to be good.

allow members to pursue the good in their own way. Classical liberals like John Stuart Mill (1806 – 1873) argued that society ought to allow all citizens to pursue their own, idiosyncratic visions of the good life. Political libertarians like Robert Nozick (1938 – 2002) argue that the state should be as small as possible to maximize freedom.

WHAT DOES SCIENCE REVEAL TO US?

At its best, science is most like...

a telescope. Realists like Ian Hacking (b. 1936) believe that science can reveal the world, serving as a kind of window into things that are microscopic or very far away.

a shovel. Instrumentalists like Bas van Fraassen (b. 1941) believe that science does not give us any special insight into what exists, but is a tool that allows to manipulate the world.

SQUARING PHILOSOPHY WITH FAITH AND SCIENCE

FAITH AND SCIENCE

When you first begin travelling in the land of ideas, you are likely to discover that your prior beliefs have some effect on your journey. If you are in love, for example, you'll find it more difficult to become an Epicurean and adopt Epicurus' austere view that love is to be avoided because it costs more in pain than you get in pleasure. Depending on what you already believe, and for reasons that may be better or worse, you are likely to avoid some areas of philosophy and prefer others.

When teaching philosophy, I found that the beliefs that constrained young philosophers usually came from two sources: from natural science or from religious faith, which in my experience meant Christianity. Very often, when confronted by conflict, apparent conflict, or even the *possibility of* conflict between faith or science on the one hand and philosophy on the other, students would abandon the philosophical question.

PHILOSOPHY AND FAITH

Christians are often suspicious of philosophy, and with some reason. Everyone knows the story of the nice Christian who goes off to college, studies philosophy and comes back as an angry atheist, having lost not only the piety that relates to God but also that which relates to family. Christians reasonably worry that this comes from a conflict between faith and philosophy.

I don't mean to minimize this concern. If Jesus Christ is, as Christians believe, the only way to eternal life, then it is not worth jeopardizing faith even for the sake of philosophy. "For what shall it profit a man," St. Mark might have asked even about friendship with wisdom, "if he shall gain the whole world, but lose his soul?"(Mark 8:36) Still, I am not sure that it is philosophy so much as the culture of the modern university that causes students to lose their faith. For universities, quite contrary to their self-image as trend setters, are in fact amplifiers of popular trends. During the British Empire, academics were enthusiastic colonialists. In the Soviet Union, they were doctrinaire communists. In fascist countries, academics were fascists. In China today, academics are nationalists. In the West, where popular culture is materialistic, irreligious and neoliberal, academics are mostly the same way.

Perhaps that's letting the study of philosophy off too easily. It is true that the dominant approach to philosophy is materialism. This is partially an effect of Immanuel Kant's (1724 – 1804) long shadow, in which philosophy stepped aside from metaphysical questions, and the place formerly occupied by metaphysics was filled by natural science. And natural science filled this role very imperfectly, because science was only designed to study physical entities and nothing beyond the physical. Since natural science has no place for entities that are not physical, and since so much of modern philosophy has given up on the project of metaphysics, the aversion to discussion of supernatural entities has passed from natural science (where it belongs) to philosophy (where it does not).

A Christian setting out to study philosophy must do so with care, and if he is setting out for university, he must take a great deal of care. Trying to understand the world is an adventure, and the outcome is not guaranteed. But the project is a Christian one, for Christianity teaches that God has invited us to become stewards of His creation. Christian doctrine does not aim at obscurity or mystery: God is reasonable, perhaps He is Reason. Christian doctrine is meant to invite and withstand the probing of someone seeking to better understand.

Christians I have met who lost their faith while studying philosophy tended to do so, not because anti-Christian arguments they encountered in philosophy were so overwhelming, but because they had stopped thinking hard about Christianity even as they developed their ideas in philosophy. The philosophical arguments they developed as young adults were coming into conflict with the understanding of faith they had developed as children of ten or twelve: it was no wonder their faith seemed shallow in comparison. Those who didn't lose their faith were active Christians, talking to other Christians, going to church, thinking about the faith and thereby updating their understanding of Christianity.

PHILOSOPHY AND SCIENCE

In the West today a quasi-religious faith tends to be placed in natural science. As I've stressed throughout this chapter, the post-Kantian withdrawal of philosophy from metaphysical questions is partly to blame for this. It creates the illusion that natural science is uniquely placed to answer our questions about how the world works.

Each philosopher must decide for himself how much weight he will give to scientific discoveries that seem to impinge on what philosophy reveals. I usually give them little weight. Because I reject the Kantian view that metaphysics is somehow off limits, most of my philosophical commitments are grounded at a level deeper than that of natural science. For example, natural science describes a world composed of material particles. Does that mean that we must be materialists? No, I think, because the metaphysical questions concern what it means to attribute existence to the very particles that natural scientists study. It may be that these particles exist within the mind, or that an immaterial structure is already presupposed in the very idea of a particle. What scientists say is usually compatible with not one but many philosophical accounts.

It is also good to keep in the back of one's mind what is sometimes called the pessimistic induction (although I do not find it so pessimistic). There have always been natural scientists, and natural scientists have always believed that the latest theory, the one they themselves believe, is the correct explanation of the physical world. But throughout history, theory after theory is replaced with new science that is sometimes better, sometimes worse, but always manages to command the faith of the next generation of natural scientists. The history of science presents us with a series of theories that everyone believed until everyone discarded them. How likely is it that it is the current year in which we have finally arrived at the truth?

For these reasons, when I am travelling in the land of ideas, I don't worry too much about whether my beliefs accord with science. I am content with a lower standard: consistency with experience. When you set out on your philosophical journey, you must decide for yourself how much confidence to place in natural science. And when you do, your journey has already begun, for that's philosophy too.

3 - APPROACHING PROBLEMS LIKE A PHILOSOPHER

PHILOSOPHERS THINK DIFFERENTLY

PRODUCT TESTERS OF IDEAS

Philosophers are always arguing about what philosophy is, but most can agree that philosophers have a way of thinking that is all our own. Philosophers have a reputation for openness to ideas and for fearless, some would say reckless debate, a reputation that goes right back to Socrates (469 – 399 BC). The philosopher David Stove (1927 – 1994), concluded his essay, "Why Have Philosophers?", with: "In argument of any kind, philosophers are *hard* men (some of whom are women), and most people do not care to tangle with us more than once or twice." I noticed this when I was a boy, growing up among philosophers. They asked questions in ways that no one else could. I wanted to be able to do it too.

Many universities offer a course in 'critical thinking', a term coined by the American philosopher John Dewey (1859 – 1952). The idea is to teach philosophical methods that students can then use in any course of study: a bit of formal and informal reasoning, a little bit of logic. These are useful tools, but they aren't what's unique to philosophical thinking. Rhetoricians and their modern-day heirs, lawyers, use the same tools to win arguments even when their position is weak, what the ancients called making the weaker argument the stronger. Philosophers like to win arguments, but we don't like making the weaker argument stronger. Historians of ideas, on the other hand, use the same tools to catalogue the shift of ideas over the course of history. Philosophers are interested in old ideas also, but only if they are philosophically defensible. Only if they might be true.

Philosophers employ the tools of logic and language in a particular way and for a particular end. We can see what that is if we think of philosophers as product testers: product testers for ideas. A product tester confronted with something to be tested needs to do two things. First, he needs to figure out what the product is for. Next, he needs to evaluate whether the product is good for that job. Applying these tests to ideas is the special trait of the philosopher.

ESTABLISHING THE PURPOSE OF THE PRODUCT

Let's start with the first step. If the product tester is given a bale of fabric, before he can decide whether it is any good, he has to know what it is supposed to do. Is it going to be made into tablecloths? Slash-resistant clothing for the military? Quick-dry clothes for campers? Biodegradable single use items? None of these purposes is objectively better or worse than any other purpose, but the answer determines what the product tester will look for. If the fabric is supposed to make hardened military wear, the product tester will try to hack through it with a knife. If it is supposed to make light, disposable hospital clothing, the knife test is unnecessary.

Philosophical ideas, like products headed for market, become testable only once we know what they are supposed to do. For example, suppose that you ask me what I think of materialism, the idea that *everything that exists is made of matter*. To test it, I would compare it to the other ideas that make up my point of view, my attempt at systematicity, which I can measure through my orientation on what I called my philosophical compass in the last chapter. In this case, I find it hard to square a belief in materialism with another belief, namely that living things have conscious immaterial minds. So if you asked me about materialism, I would test it by thinking about minds.

How does the idea that everything is matter explain the existence of conscious minds? Can you make a mind out of matter?

Just as product testing without a defined purpose would be pointless, doing philosophy without orienting yourself on a philosophical compass is impossible. But your orientation can be temporary or provisional. Product testers don't necessarily use the products they test. The product tester who is testing a mattress may be perfectly happy with his own mattress. But he puts himself in the position of someone who needs a new mattress for the duration of the test. In the same way, when you do philosophy, you may test an idea from someone else's point of view. Take again the idea that everything is matter. I think that's false, but I might imagine that it was true, and adjust my philosophical compass for that position. Then I can find out what the world looks like to a materialist.

CHOOSING THE RIGHT TESTS FOR THE PRODUCT

Once a product tester knows what an item is supposed to do, he is ready for the second step. He has to actually test the item. If the product is a candy that is supposed to taste like strawberries, perhaps the test consists of offering it to a number of people to see whether they all taste a strawberry flavour. If the product is a screen that is foldable, perhaps the test consists of folding it thousands of times to see whether it begins to crack. Part of the product tester's art is to choose tests that will correctly simulate use. If a major flaw is not discovered until the product has been mass produced, the product tester has failed.

You can't test an idea without putting it through its paces, but important as it is, this is the step that philosophers often struggle to explain. When faced with a conceptual product, philosophers develop, partly through study and analysis, partly through experience, a sense of where to flex it and squeeze it and put it under pressure to see whether it will crack or hold up. The more conceptual products you test, the better at it you'll become, but there are three main ways that philosophers test an idea.

How we Test Ideas

SIMULATING DAILY USE

The first test for philosophical ideas is to get as close as possible to the conditions of daily use. Every product is going to be used in some context. For example, a camp stove may work very well in a laboratory, but to be of use it needs to work in wind and rain. Therefore, the stove must be tested in windy and rainy environments. Until you have done so, you won't know if the camp stove is any good.

Philosophy always risks a certain remove from everyday life. Simulating daily use is a way of taking ideas out of the clean laboratory of philosophy and considering them in messy real-life situations. Is this account of human motivation psychologically plausible? Does anyone really think that?

One of the most striking recent examples of a failure to take philosophy out of the lab is the case of the late philosophy professor Herbert Fingarette (1921 – 2018). Fingarette wrote a book called *Death: Philosophical Soundings* (1999), where he noted the irrationality of fearing death, which he believed was the annihilation of the person. Since death means being gone, you'll never have to experience it. What's to fear? This idea seems good in the sterile laboratory of philosophy, but much less so in real life. Shortly before his death, Fingarette allowed his son to make him the star of a sad little documentary called *Being 97*. Facing his own death, Fingarette was sorry to learn that his previous arguments provided him with no comfort. He was uncertain and afraid.

Fingarette's argument was an adaptation of an Epicurean argument, but I doubt that Epicurus (341 – 270 BC) would have found Fingarette's results surprising. Epicurus recognized that his argument was more than an argument, that it was in fact part of a 'fourfold cure' (discussed in more detail in the last chapter) which played a therapeutic as well as philosophical role. In the same way, both Christianity and Buddhism have recognized that preparation for death is a matter of conditioning our minds, not just of changing our beliefs, the way developing a strong body demands constant exercise, not merely good intentions.

COMPARING OTHER PRODUCTS

Product testers generally learn about other products similar to the one they are testing. This research can help to establish the niche for the product being tested. Does it do what other products do, but better? Does it do the same thing, but in a different area?

Philosophers too can benefit from testing ideas by comparison to other ideas that are structurally similar. Philosophers, for example, like to consider ancient democracies to test our own moment. On the internet, where everyone can put forward an opinion, mobs quickly develop and demand sweeping changes. When trying to understand where this volatility can lead, we remember the Athenian experiment with direct democracy. The Athenian people could vote on anything, and a majority carried the vote. As a result, on one occasion, they voted to execute most of their elected government, and promptly did so. Often after a controversial vote, the electorate had second thoughts and voted to harshly punish the instigators of such votes, as also happened shortly afterward. The parallel to the erratic behaviour of an electronic mob is not hard to see, and so we might consider Athenian democracy to help us understand mobs on the internet. Philosophers call this 'argument by analogy'. It is one of the most powerful and versatile philosophical tools that we have.

CREATING EXTREME CONDITIONS

Another way to find out whether a product will break under normal conditions is to try using it in extraordinary conditions first. To find out if something can survive a light drop, you throw it off a high building. To see if it will melt on a hot day you put it over a flame. If the product survives the test, you can rest assured that it will not break under ordinary usage.

Philosophers simulate extreme conditions by looking for limit cases: the smallest and the largest, the widest and the narrowest, the most complete and the least complete. When given a rule, the philosopher tests that rule against the most extreme case he can think of. If the rule survives this extreme testing, it is likely to work under less extreme circumstances. In the second chapter, we saw that Hellenistic philosophers wondered whether the wise man can be happy if he is tortured to death. They had a good eye for extreme cases.

We can see the value in considering extreme cases in that old question, *what separates man from beast?* It's tempting to reply that the difference is a certain level of intelligence, or rationality, or self-awareness. However, the weakness of such an answer becomes apparent when you consider the extreme cases: not an average animal and an average human being, but the most outstanding animal and the least developed human being. Compare retarded people, young children, or the senile to very clever animals and we see that it is not so obvious that every human being is more intelligent, rational, or self aware than every animal.

One side effect of learning to think in terms of extreme cases is that you will begin to notice that in ordinary language, we use superlatives to add emphasis. We say that this is the kindest act, or the most beautiful girl, when all we really mean is that that the act is kind and the girl is beautiful. To philosophers, especially those just getting used to philosophy, these superlatives begin to stand out. Young philosophers sometimes develop the annoying habit of pouncing on them.

"Going to get ice cream," someone might say, "is the best idea ever!"

"Really," replies the young philosopher, "the *best* idea *ever*? What about the wheel? What about the idea that surgeons should wash their hands before operations? What about peace on earth? Aren't *those* better ideas?"

Noticing superlatives is a good sign, because it shows that you are thinking like a product tester. Constantly pointing them out, however, is unlikely to win you many friends. It is *infinitely* irritating.

PHILOSOPHICAL PRODUCT TESTING IN ACTION

EPICUREAN FREEDOM: THE ACCOUNT

Now that we have seen the three things a product tester does, we can put them into action on a single philosophical idea. Epicurus (341 – 270 BC) taught that humans possess freedom, what we would nowadays call 'free will'. He was a materialist, believing that everything consists of atoms and space. Usually atoms behave in deterministic ways: they move because another atom bumped them, and the one that bumped them moved because of a previous atom, and the chain of causation goes all the way back to the beginning, wherever that was. However, atoms occasionally act in a random way: for no reason at all, they swerve. This random swerve is the key to Epicurus' understanding of freedom.

Epicurus was worried about determinism. When you watch a Rube Goldberg machine in action, some small event like a dropped marble prompts a long sequence of surprising and delighting consequences. The machine is interesting, but it isn't free. Are we like that? Are our experiences and beliefs just like marbles activating the very complicated machine of our brains and bodies so that we react in ways that may be surprising to others but are in truth totally deterministic? Epicurus thought not, and that swerves in the brain could help us to understand why. (Strictly speaking, Epicurus would say that the swerve occurs not in the brain, but in the part of you that thinks, which he understood as like a mist that permeates the body. For our purposes, we can update Epicurus slightly and just say 'the brain'.)

Even though Epicurus wrote many books, they are for the most part lost to history, and so the best and fullest description of what he meant by freedom is preserved in a book length piece of poetry written, in Latin, to celebrate the Epicurean philosophy. Here's how the Roman Epicurean poet Lucretius (died around 55 BC) put it:

> And so, if motion is always interconnected, and new motion comes from old motion in a fixed order, nor do the first things [he means atoms], through a swerve, effect some beginning of motion and break the laws of fate, so that cause should not follow cause from infinity, then whence comes the freedom of living things throughout the world, whence, I say, comes this will torn away from fate by which we go each where pleasure leads, [and] swerve our motions, not at any given time or place, but where the

mind itself leads? (Lucretius, *De Rerum Natura*, my translation 2.251-260)

Here's what most people think Lucretius is saying. Suppose that a man is trying to decide between two courses of action, A and B. What makes him free? Well, he is free because a random swerve could occur in his brain such that he would choose A, or a totally different but still random swerve could occur in his brain such that he would choose B. The man's choice would not be caused by deterministic processes, because it would be caused by a random atomic swerve instead. Most of the man's thinking is caused by deterministic processes, yes, but his choice of A and B could be free if a swerve makes him do A or B. This is how most people read Epicurus, and that was true even in antiquity, where the Neoplatonic philosopher Plotinus (204/5 – 270 AD) explicitly attacked the view that I have just described.

EPICUREAN FREEDOM: PRODUCT PURPOSE

The first thing we need to do when testing this idea is to become oriented. Where does Epicurus fall on our compass? Two of the cardinal directions will be relevant here. On the question, what is the universe made of, Epicurus is a materialist. The universe is made of atoms and void, nothing else. On the question of whether man is free, Epicurus is a metaphysical libertarian, and so he answers yes. Our freedom is incompatible with the determinism that characterizes other things. Water flowing downhill, for example, is not free, because it follows deterministic processes. But man is not like that. Man is free because of the atomic swerves in his brain.

Now that we are oriented, we see how this account has to work. Because we are operating as materialists, we cannot appeal to anything outside of the body. Because we are operating as metaphysical libertarians, we have to show how human decision making is different from ordinary causal processes. Using only physical processes, we need to spell out a plausible account of human freedom. These are the terms on which Epicurus' account will succeed or fail.

EPICUREAN FREEDOM: DAILY USE

One of the questions we can ask is whether a philosophical theory accounts for everyday experience. So take a case of free action: a young man agonizes for a while, as young men do, and finally asks a girl to go out with him. The young man thinks about whether it is the right time, worries about what the girl might say, and finally screws up his courage. He could have decided not to go ahead and could have chickened out, but he doesn't. If any of the young man's choices are free, this one is.

According to the view we are considering, the young man is free because after all his agonizing, a random swerve occurred in his brain that made him decide that now is the time to ask the girl to go out with him. But does that describe this experience? Free decisions aren't characterized by a cognitive break where randomness takes over. What was the point of screwing up his courage if the random swerve was what actually made him do it? The model, it seems, does a poor job of describing everyday experience.

EPICUREAN FREEDOM: COMPARISON

Another way to test the Epicurean model of free will is to compare it to something else, to seek out the same structure elsewhere. How could we analogize the random swerving of an atom in the brain? Well, let's imagine the brain is much bigger than it is so that we can see inside it: let's imagine the brain as a company. A company realizes it is locked into a certain pattern of decision making. Desperate to break out, the company hires a consultant and tells him that he is to act like a free agent. The company entrusts the decisions to the consultant; whatever he recommends the company will do. The consultant reviews all the company's previous decision making and makes a decision the company would not have made.

This seems analogous to a random swerve producing a decision that you would not otherwise have reached. But it also shows the problem with the Epicurean account. In the case of the company and the consultant, we would not say that the company reached the decision. Rather, they hired someone else to reach the decision for them. That's the whole point of the consultant! Now, in the case of the Epicurean theory of free will, the random swerve of the atom has nothing to do with you. You didn't make it happen; it's external to your mind, a foreign influence coming in and making the decision for you. So if you wouldn't say that *the company* made the decision when they bring in the consultant, neither should you say that *you* make the decision when an atom swerves in your brain.

EPICUREAN FREEDOM: EXTREME CONDITIONS

Finally, let's try to push the Epicurean product to an extreme. According to the view we are testing, freedom is a random atomic swerve. So consider some limit cases. What if you only get one swerve per lifetime? Or, better yet, what if every single decision you make your whole life long is free? That seems possible, if unlikely. Now in that case, every single decision would be the result of a random atomic motion. What would that be like? Our philosophical compass reminds us that we have to spell this out in materialist terms. That means that, no matter what experiences you have or memories you have built up, those exist as physical states of your brain. The atomic swerve is random, meaning that it is not connected to any of those physical states. And so, the freer you are, the more disconnected you will be from your memory and experience. Total freedom would mean total randomness, and would mean that what you do is completely disconnected from any typical way of doing things that people would call your character. The person who is free at every moment would be a puppet of randomness. That seems absurd.

That is, in fact, the point that Plotinus makes against his reading of Epicurus. Here's how Plotinus put it in his typical dense and difficult style:

> Causelessness is quite inadmissible; we can make no place here for unwarranted 'slantings,' for sudden movement of bodies apart from any initiating power, for precipitate spurts in a soul with nothing to drive it into the new course of action. ... Such causelessness would bind the Soul under an even sterner compulsion, no longer master of itself, but at the mercy of movements apart from will and cause. (Plotinus, *Enneads*, translated by Stephen Mackenna and B. S. Page 3.1.1.)

Plotinus is saying that we cannot understand the process of choice as boiling down to the random occurrence of a 'slanting', i.e. an atomic swerve, because of the *causelessness* (we'd probably say *randomness*) of the swerves. What he means is that the randomness of the swerve is a kind of compulsion.

Determinism seems like compulsion, but the random swerve is no better.

As we saw, Lucretius is delighted by the prospect of 'freedom torn away from fate'. But that's not so exciting if freedom turns out to be compulsion too, just random compulsion. Better to be a puppet of fate, you might think, than a puppet of randomness: at least fate works through our characters.

EPICUREAN FREEDOM: CONCLUSION

We set out to test a product: an Epicurean account of freedom. The account states that random atomic motion *is* free choice. We found this unpersuasive. It failed all three tests. It doesn't translate to the messiness of ordinary life. In analogous cases, the account does not work. And when we pushed the account to the limit, it broke down.

The Epicurean account does not pass basic product testing. It is a flawed theory, and deserves to be rejected. If Epicurus believed this – and although it is a common reading, I'm not convinced that he did – then so much the worse for him, he was wrong.

WORKING WITH ANOTHER PRODUCT TESTER

DIALECTIC

Up until now I have written about the way a lone philosopher approaches problems. But philosophy is a social activity. Philosophers like arguing with one another and solving problems together. This joint activity is what Plato (429 – 347 BC) and Aristotle (384 – 322 BC) called dialectic. So let us consider how product testing works when there are two or more product testers working together.

Plato and Aristotle thought that dialectic is the most fundamental method of philosophy. One reason for this is that philosophers have a problem that product testers don't, namely that the quality of a product is only what you make of it. If a product tester drops a piece of electronics off a building to see if it can withstand the fall, gravity and the quality of the electronics will deliver a result. But when you bring an objection to an idea, it's also up to you to provide the best counter-objection that you can think of. Ideas are passive and inert. You, the philosopher, have to make them resistant to your tests.

Plato shows us how to work with other philosophers in his dialogues, choosing to present his own thoughts through the mouth of his teacher, Socrates (469 – 399 BC). It's likely that Plato started writing dialogues after Socrates was condemned to death, in part for the activities the dialogues describe. As Plato reports, Socrates met and spoke with various well-known and powerful Athenians who claimed to be experts in their fields. Euthyphro, a priest, claimed to understand the nature of piety. The generals Laches and Nicias claim to understand the nature of courage. Socrates' careful and ironic questions collapsed their façades of knowledge, and the humiliated experts hurried off or reluctantly admitted their ignorance.

Why did Socrates do this? Plato tells us that Socrates, when he was younger, was troubled by his own ignorance, and so sent a message to the oracle of the god Apollo asking for help.

"Who is the wisest man in Athens?" Socrates asked the god.

The answer came back: "You are."

Socrates was puzzled. His discomfort with his own ignorance had prompted his question in the first place. He knew he wasn't wise. But it is not in the character of a god to lie or make mistakes. So Socrates decided to seek clarification. He would find someone who was wiser than he was, then go back to the oracle and point to this man and ask for an explanation. Socrates turned Athens upside down looking for that wise man. And as Socrates' questions exposed the ignorance of every new candidate, Socrates slowly began to understand the oracle. Socrates' wisdom, such as it was, consisted in understanding his ignorance. But more than that, when Socrates had gone to the god with a question, the god had provided much more than an answer. Apollo had made Socrates his instrument, and through Socrates created the discipline and method of philosophy, where answers to Socratic questions might be sought and found. For Socrates, the god's mission ended in a death sentence for religious dissent and corrupting the youth: a thinly veiled way of saying that he humiliated many famous men and they had enough of it. But the discipline and method that the god created through Socrates lived on. That is why, even though Socrates was not the first philosopher, we call him the father of philosophy today.

Socrates described dialectic as consisting of two roles: asking and answering. The person asking is the one applying tests to the product. When Euthyphro and Laches and Nicias claim to know something they naturally take on the role of answering questions. Socrates does the asking. In the course of the dialectic, their definitions unravel under Socrates' questions, much as we saw the position attributed to Epicurus unravel above. In the end, the products don't pass the test.

As Plato himself grew more confident in his own views, he put them into the mouth of Socrates. This marks the passage from what are called Plato's early to his middle dialogues. In the middle dialogues, the most famous of which is *The Republic*, the experts suggest ideas that mostly fail, but now Socrates is suggesting ideas of his own, and these do not fail. To get Plato's masterclass in dialectic, we will need to turn to the early and middle dialogues. There we can learn both how to ask a question, and how to answer one.

COMPETING WITH ANOTHER PRODUCT TESTER

It is the middle dialogues where both Socrates and his interlocutors enter the dialectic with a position to defend, each with a product to test. In this case, the product testing becomes competitive: each tester wants to defend his product while showing that the other's product is flawed. This is the normal structure of an argument in philosophy. But it is worth remembering that, as in the Socratic dialogues, only one product can be tested at a time. Showing that your opponent is wrong doesn't mean you're right. Your product might be a dud too.

University programs in philosophy today tend to downplay the competitive nature of argument, and that is a mistake. Arguments are better and more fun when you attack your opponent's product with everything you've got. But you can't just be having fun. You have to be disciplined and stick to testing the product. If you do, every encounter sharpens you and prepares you for the next one.

Arguing to win means that sometimes you are going to lose. But even when you lose a philosophical argument, you can gain from the encounter. Arguing is a little bit like boxing or martial arts. Yes, it's nice to be stronger and better and faster than the other fellow, but it's possible to fail in all these respects and still walk away with a wealth of new knowledge and tricks. Socrates was always saying that he was happy to lose an argument, because win or lose, his own thinking would be clarified. When that happens, for it will, you now have the task of fitting what you learned into the rest of what you believe.

Unfortunately, not everyone can be as easygoing as Socrates at the prospect of losing an argument. In my experience, people who lose an argument very rarely say, "You were right and I was wrong". Arguments, even in philosophy, usually end quietly with a change of topic. This is how the person who can no longer answer keeps his dignity. In Plato's early dialogues, Socrates wants more, he wants his interlocutor to admit that he was wrong. Socrates' trick was to argue in front of an audience. When the expert suddenly couldn't think of an answer, the boos and jeers of the audience kept him from changing the topic or walking away. Making sure that you have an audience is a good way to establish who won the argument. But as

Socrates' fate reminds us, it is not a very good way to make friends.

4 – EXPRESSING YOURSELF LIKE A PHILOSOPHER

TAKING RESPONSIBILITY FOR WORDS

ON STYLE AND CONTENT

There is one thing that sets philosophical writing apart from other kinds of writing: philosophers take responsibility for their words. No matter how beautiful or how plain a passage of philosophy may be, the philosopher has chosen his words carefully so as to display his ideas. As we saw in the last chapter, philosophers are like product testers. When a philosopher expresses himself, he is using the logic that is inside ordinary language to get the product ready for testing.

When you use language to present a philosophical idea, you need to make sure your language is simple and clear so that you and your audience can see the logical structure. You are the architect of your ideas, and you must ensure that the structure will stand up and not collapse. Just this achievement will give your work a kind of beauty, but so far it will only be visible to your fellow philosophers. Some philosophers are content with this. If you want to see the work of a philosophical architect who builds for his fellow architects, you can do no better than the *Summa Theologica* of St. Thomas Aquinas (1225 – 1274). Aquinas' arguments are clear and simple, and there are no distracting stylistic elements. But it must be said that one reason that Aquinas wrote the way that he did was that he was writing inside the university, for other scholars. His audience of professionals didn't want to be distracted by a fancy façade. In the same way, the writings of contemporary scholars are often formulaic and rarely beautiful. It is philosophy written for those who have a professional obligation to read or at least skim it.

If you decide to write or talk about philosophy, you may not have a captive audience, and if you don't, you can look to philosophers who worked outside the university. Plato (429 – 347 BC) built up an audience that has lasted more than two thousand years with his beautiful presentations of Socrates in action. Michel de Montaigne (1533 – 1592) invented the philosophical essay, a form that at its best combines philosophical rigour and literary litheness to bend

itself around the edges of the human condition.
Montaigne said he wrote for his friends, but countless
readers have been drawn in by his beautiful writing.
The Empiricists, namely John Locke (1632 – 1704),
George Berkeley (1685 –1753) and David Hume (1711
– 1776), were united not only by the view that all
knowledge comes from experience (*empereia*, in
Greek), but also by their commitment to writing
philosophy in clear and beautifully crafted English. In
what follows, we will look at a passage of David
Hume's in which he lays out his famous 'riddle of
induction', and does so without compromising on style.
The novelist George Orwell had six rules of writing
well. We will find seven beautifully executed rules of
philosophical writing in Hume. But first we need to set
the scene.

Seven Rules of Philosophical Writing

Hume's scepticism

In *An Enquiry Concerning Human Understanding*,
Hume makes a surprising observation. We see things
we call *causes* joined with things we call *effects*; the
cause happens, and then the effect happens. But we
don't see what connects the one to the other. When we
go looking for the causality that underlies the world,
we do not find it. Dropped stones fall. Babies grow up
into adults. The sun rises in the East every morning.

But we don't see the causal power that makes any of these things happen.

The problem is that the dropped stone and the falling stone are two different things. We get used to seeing the one lead to the other, but if you asked what *makes* the one lead to the other, Hume thinks that we have no answer. You might respond that the reason the stone falls is the law of gravity. But a 'law' is just a regularity. Gravity doesn't *make* anything happen, it is just a description of *how* things happen. A physicist or some other scientist might have a very precise explanation of the laws at work when the stone is dropped. But if you asked him why laws work this way and not some other way, he would likely shrug and tell you to ask a philosopher.

I find it helpful to think of Hume's point through the medium of video. Suppose you see a video clip of someone releasing a stone, which then falls from his hand. In this case, the stone isn't falling because of gravity. It's falling because of the director's choices. That's because the video clip of the stone being released is one thing, and the video clip of the stone falling is another, and there's no reason one has to follow from the other. Instead of showing the stone falling, the director could have added a special effects scene of the stone flying away or exploding, or he could have cut to something else entirely. But here's the thing: when the director does show the stone falling in the video, don't you see exactly what you would see if you saw a stone dropped in real life? We *know* that in the video, there's no causality to be found. Since there's no causality to be found in the video, and since there's nothing additional to experience in real life, it seems that causality is not something we experience.

So we do not experience causality, and it seems that all we can say of it is that it applies regularly. But how can we be sure it will continue to apply regularly? Can we know anything about the natural world with certainty? When Hume first asked himself this question and realized he had no answer, it sent him into a depression, and when he recovered he did so as a sceptic, not setting too much stock in certainty. It was also this argument that awoke Immanuel Kant (1724 – 1804), as he said, from his dogmatic slumber. Kant was so desperate to escape Hume's scepticism that he built a philosophical account around the lack of an answer, an account on which we can never understand things as they are in themselves.

It is against this background that the passage we are about to read is written. Hume makes his argument by distinguishing between 'sensible qualities' and 'secret powers'. The sensible qualities of the stone are its heaviness, shape, and colour. Secret power is causal power, the secret (because we don't know what it is) explanation for why stones regularly fall when dropped. In Hume's terms, the question is how you can know that certain sensible qualities will act as usual since you don't know their secret powers. What makes you think that this time, when the stone is dropped, the secret powers will kick in? How do you know that the present will continue to resemble the past? You might reply that we have established this by experimentation, by natural science. That's where our quotation from Hume picks up. I'll present what he says – only one paragraph – and then we'll take it apart piece by piece to find Hume's seven rules.

> Should it be said that, from a number of uniform experiments, we infer a connection between the sensible qualities and the secret powers: this, I must confess, seems the same difficulty, couched in different terms. The question still recurs, on what process of argument this inference is founded? Where is the medium, the interposing ideas, which join propositions so very wide of each other? From a body of like colour and consistence with bread we expect like nourishment and support. But this surely is a step or progress of the mind, which wants to be explained. When a man says, "I have found, in all past instances, such sensible qualities conjoined with such secret powers," and when he says, "Similar sensible qualities will always be conjoined with similar secret powers," he is not guilty of a tautology, nor are these propositions in any respect the same. You say that the one proposition is an inference from the other. But

you must confess that the inference is not intuitive, neither is it demonstrative. Of what nature is it, then? To say it is experimental, is begging the question. For all inferences from experience suppose, as their foundation, that the future will resemble the past, and that similar powers will be conjoined with similar sensible qualities. If there be any suspicion that the course of nature may change, and that the past may be no rule for the future, all experience becomes useless, and can give rise to no inference or conclusion. It is impossible, therefore, that any arguments from experience can prove this resemblance of the past to the future, since all these arguments are founded on the supposition of that resemblance. Let the course of things be allowed hitherto ever so regular; that alone, without some new argument or inference, proves not that, for the future, it will continue so. In vain do you pretend to have learned the nature of bodies from your past experience. Their secret nature, and consequently all their effects and influence, may change, without any change in their sensible qualities. This happens sometimes, and with regard to some objects; why may it not happen always, and with regard to all objects? What logic, what process of argument secures you against this supposition? My practice, you say, refutes my doubts. But you mistake the purport of my question. As an agent, I am quite satisfied in the point; but as a philosopher, who has some share of curiosity, I will not say scepticism, I want to learn the foundation of this inference. No reading, no enquiry has yet been able to remove my difficulty, or give me satisfaction in a matter of such importance. Can I do better than propose the difficulty to the public, even though, perhaps, I have small hopes of obtaining a solution? We shall at least, by this means, be sensible of our ignorance, if we do not augment our knowledge. (David Hume, *An Enquiry Concerning Human Understanding* 4.2)

It's a long passage, and even though Hume is a very clear writer, we will learn more by breaking the passage into smaller pieces. Breaking one complex thing into many simpler things is a part of the scientific method, but it applies to philosophy as well, which is perhaps not so surprising, since the scientific method was invented by a philosopher. So we have already arrived at our first rule:

RULE 1: BREAK LARGE, COMPLEX PROBLEMS INTO SMALLER, SIMPLER ONES.

So how do we break down Hume's paragraph here?

STATING THE THESIS

The first thing to do is to find out what Hume is trying to persuade us about, namely to find the thesis of Hume's argument. Hume makes it easy for us by stating his thesis up front. There is only one small complication: Hume is stating a sceptical thesis. He's not trying to show us something, he's trying to show us that we don't know what perhaps we thought we did know.

Remember, Hume is addressing a reader who has already read that we cannot observe the secret power, causality. The imaginary reader has replied that we learn about the secret power through experimentation, by trial and error. When Hume begins, "Should it be said that," he's imagining you or someone else making this argument. Hume's sceptical thesis is that even if you make this argument, you still haven't solved his problem, because you still can't be sure that causes will lead to effects.

> **Sceptical Thesis:** Should it be said that, from a number of uniform experiments, we infer a connection between the sensible qualities and the secret powers: **this**, I must confess, **seems the same difficulty, couched in different terms**. The question still recurs, on what process of argument this inference is founded? Where is the medium, the interposing ideas, which join propositions so very wide of each other?

I bolded the actual words of Hume's thesis, which are very simple. If you think that experimental science can help you to escape Hume's scepticism, you are wrong, because you are really just restating the same view that Hume has already put in question. The remainder of the paragraph will support this thesis, but before we see how let us note a second rule of philosophical writing from Hume:

RULE 2: CLEARLY EXPRESS A THESIS *UP FRONT.*

Rule 2 is one of the hardest things for young philosophers to learn. One reason why stating a thesis can be difficult is that it is a form of intellectual self-discipline. The thesis will constrain what you can say and prevent you from rambling. Stating a thesis can also feel like you are giving away the ending, as though spoiling a book or a movie. In a story, the ending is what matters. Philosophy is not like that. The really important part of philosophy is the journey, the argument. Your reader or listener will be better able to follow the argument if he knows where it is leading.

In the paragraph that we are looking at, Hume's thesis is broad: natural science will not help you to escape scepticism. Hume argues for narrower theses in other parts of his book. Both of Hume's empiricist predecessors, John Locke (1632 – 1704) and George Berkeley (1685 – 1753), did think they had an experience of the supposedly secret power of causality, so Hume presents more specific arguments against them to show why they were mistaken.

Those starting in philosophy often have trouble narrowing their theses, so that you often end up trying to prove much more than you can prove. Unless you have to write an essay for a course, you probably don't need to pick a thesis, so you can wait for something to come along that you believe and then write or talk about that. But if you do find yourself in need of something to say, the best place to look is a disagreement between philosophers. Hume is attacking Berkeley and Locke. Is his attack successful? If not, why not? If so, why did Berkeley and Locke not anticipate it? If you can find an answer to one of these questions, you will have an interesting and narrow thesis.

USING EXAMPLES

The next thing that Hume does is to stop and illustrate his point with an example. As we saw in the previous chapter, when you are testing an idea, one way to do it is to apply it to an ordinary situation to see if it still makes sense. Often, that will mean giving an example. It's also a good exercise to provide your own examples when you are reading or hearing about someone else's ideas, to stop and consider whether you can spell them out. Hume does this by thinking about the experience of buying bread at the bakery.

Example: From a body of like colour and consistence with bread we expect like nourishment and support. But this surely is a step or progress of the mind, which wants [in modern English, we would not say 'wants' but 'needs'] to be explained.

If you have ever bought bread at a bakery, you have made the inference, the 'step or progress of the mind', that Hume is describing, although it is probably so quick and instinctive that you don't even notice you're doing it. You must think to yourself, "That looks like a nice loaf of bread. Bread has always nourished me before. So I think this bread will nourish me too." You don't think the bread will poison you, or go through your system offering no nutrients, or set you on fire... if you thought any of those things you wouldn't buy it or eat it. Hume's point is that even here, we have the problematic assumption that the future will continue in the way of the past. All you know is that in the past, bread was nourishing. That doesn't prove it will be today. So here is our third rule from Hume:

RULE 3: WHENEVER SOMETHING IS COMPLICATED OR ABSTRACT, GIVE AN EXAMPLE.

A well-chosen example like Hume's will illustrate a point while also showing you why you should care. Every time you look at a piece of food, you make the inference that Hume is describing. If Hume is right, you are literally making this mistake at breakfast, lunch and dinner.

FRAMING

You can choose more than just your thesis when you present an idea, you can also choose how to frame it. This is, in effect, choosing the philosophical terrain where you want to fight. A talented opponent may try to move you to terrain that is more favourable to him, but since you are setting up the discussion, you have first pick. As we will see in a moment, Hume is a master of framing the issue, but first let's note the rule:

RULE 4: FRAME YOUR QUESTION OR TOPIC SO YOUR ARGUMENTS WILL SUPPORT YOUR THESIS.

Hume's topic is in metaphysics. He could have framed the issue as the question of what causality could possibly be. Or he could have framed it, as I did above when talking about a video, as a question of experience: what does one experience when one sees a stone dropped? Instead, Hume frames the problem as a question of logic.

> **Framing:** When a man says, "I have found, in all past instances, such sensible qualities conjoined with such secret powers," and when he says, "Similar sensible qualities will always be conjoined with similar secret powers," he is not

4 - Expressing Yourself like a Philosopher

guilty of a tautology, nor are these propositions in any respect the same.

Up to now, we found that certain sensible qualities (for example bread) had secret powers (bread nourished us). The question is whether this statement about the past contains an insight about the future. A tautology is an empty statement that is necessarily true. It doesn't matter what A symbolizes, you already know that A = A, because "A = A" is a tautology. By contrast, A = B is not a tautology, for it could be true or false. Hume is saying that when someone goes from this:

> **the past:** I have found, in all past instances, such sensible qualities conjoined with such secret powers

to this:

> **a prediction:** Similar sensible qualities will always be conjoined with similar secret powers

it is *not* a tautology. The logical value of the proposition I'm calling 'a prediction' is not contained in the logical value of 'the past'. But obviously, when we buy bread and expect it to nourish us, we are going from the past to a prediction. How are we getting there? There are, as we are about to find out, three possibilities.

THE ARGUMENT

Hume opens his argument by considering these three possibilities, or to use the jargon of philosophy, he opens with a trilemma. Usually when someone presents a trilemma, a forced choice between three options, (a dilemma is a choice between just two), he is going to show you that there is something wrong with all but one choice, so that is the one you must choose.

> **Trilemma:** You say that the one proposition is an inference from the other. But you must confess that the inference is not intuitive, neither is it demonstrative. Of what nature is it, then? To say it is experimental, is begging the question. For all inferences from experience suppose, as their foundation, that the future will resemble the past, and that similar powers will be conjoined with similar sensible qualities.

You, the imaginary objector have claimed that you can get from the past to a prediction. That means you're making an inference. There are three kinds of inferences you might be making. You could be making (1) an intuitive inference, (2) a demonstrative inference, or (3) an experimental inference. We are going to choose (3) an experimental inference, but Hume wants to show you that you actually don't have a free choice: (3) is your only choice. By showing this, Hume is closing the exits and stopping you from going back to change your mind and choose another option.

The first option is that the inference from the past to a prediction is intuitive. An intuitive inference is something that you can infer without even reasoning. For example, a tautology is an intuitive inference. You don't reason your way to the conclusion that A = A, you know it already without even needing to think about it. But as Hume has already said, this isn't a tautology. A claim about the past doesn't automatically lead to a prediction. So this can't be an intuitive inference.

The second option is that that we are looking at a demonstrative inference. An example of a demonstrative inference is the inference that if cats are mammals and Felix is a cat, Felix must be a mammal. It's not obvious in the same way as an intuitive inference is obvious, because you have to reason your way through it. But once you do that, you can see that it must be true that if cats are mammals and Felix is a cat, Felix is also a mammal. Is it true in the same way that once you have understood the implications of the past you automatically get to a prediction? Hume doesn't think so. We can imagine a science fiction scenario where today is the day that bread stops nourishing us. We can't imagine a science fiction scenario where all cats are mammals and Felix is a cat, but today Felix is *not* a mammal.

The only other option, Hume thinks, is that this is experimental reasoning, or as we would say today, 'inductive reasoning'. That is why the argument that we are about to see is sometimes called Hume's riddle of induction. So the heart of the argument is directed against induction.

> **Argument:** If there be any suspicion that the course of nature may change, and that the past may be no rule for the future, all experience becomes useless, and can give rise to no inference or conclusion. It is impossible, therefore, that any arguments from experience can prove this resemblance of the past to the future, since all these arguments are founded on the supposition of that resemblance.

In more modern English, what Hume is saying is that if you don't independently know that a prediction follows from the past, then experience alone can't bring you to that conclusion. Next he observes that you don't independently know that a prediction follows from the past. And so he concludes that experience can't help you arrive at this conclusion. The form of argument that Hume uses here is one of the most common logical structures. Medieval philosophers named it *modus ponens*, which means the strong mode. *Modus ponens* works like this:

Premise 1: If A then B.

Premise 2: A

Conclusion: Therefore, B

Although Hume is too artful a writer to repeat himself, that is what is going on in the passage above. Here is the same passage again, with the pieces labelled.

> **Modus Ponens: ({Premise 1}** If there be any suspicion that the course of nature may change, and that the past may be no rule for the future, all experience becomes useless, and can give rise to no inference or conclusion.) (**{Conclusion}** It is impossible, therefore, that any arguments from experience can prove this resemblance of the past to the future), since (**{Premise 2}** all these arguments are founded on the supposition of that resemblance).

As we see, Hume's final premise comes after the conclusion. In written or spoken philosophy, although arguments tend to be grouped together they are not always explained sequentially. As a reader or listener, you will have to spell out the logical structure for yourself.

Modus ponens has a good, working logical structure, or to use the technical term for a well-built argument, it is *valid*. This technical term comes from the Latin *validus* which means powerful, robust or healthy. Any argument that has the structure of *modus ponens* is valid. A valid argument doesn't necessarily lead you to truth in your conclusion, however. The structure is sound, but that won't help you if you start with false assumptions in your premises. Here's a nonsense argument to show you what I mean: if my neighbour Bill has legs then Bill has a tail. Bill does have legs, so he must have a tail. The argument is valid, which we can tell because it has the form of *modus ponens*, but its first premise is false. Plenty of animals, including all humans, have legs but no tails. Validity doesn't make an argument true. Rather, validity will preserve truth, by which I mean that if the premises are true and the argument is valid, the conclusion must be true also.

When we say that an argument is good, we usually mean that the argument is valid *and also* that the premises are true. The technical term for this in philosophy is *soundness*: a sound argument is valid *and* has true premises. This means that a sound argument always has a true conclusion. Here is our next rule of philosophical writing:

RULE 5: MAKE YOUR ARGUMENT SOUND.

Since every sound argument is valid, the only question for us is whether Hume's argument is sound.

Remember, we went looking for a way to get from a fact about the past to a prediction about the future. And because Hume is arguing in *modus ponens*, and the second premise repeats part of the first premise, we really need to know whether the opening conditional proposition is true. Is it true that *if you don't independently know that a prediction follows from the past, then experience alone can't allow you to reach that conclusion?* That seems correct: the experimental method is based on the assumption that repeated experiments will show you a pattern that you can generalize and apply to future cases. Hume's scepticism puts the whole experimental method in doubt. That's why an experimental answer won't do: it's presupposing the very thing that Hume doubts.

Some readers find Hume's rejection of experimentation unsatisfying. We're so reliant on experimental reasoning that it's hard to see how it could fail us. We imagine natural scientists scoffing at Hume's worries. If you feel this way, consider the case of a particularly clever turkey. Every day, the farmer comes out and feeds the turkey. Gradually, the turkey notices a pattern. Perhaps the turkey is even something of a scientist, so it reasons that this pattern of feedings indicates that in the future the farmer will come out and feed it again. And until Thanksgiving, the pattern holds.

The turkey was right to notice a pattern of events in the past. Its mistake was to assume that the pattern meant that on Thanksgiving morning, it was going to get food instead of being food. It was missing the motivation of the pattern, the why. The turkey thought the pattern was new day, then new food, repeating forever. We recognize a more complex pattern, the pattern that we call 'fattening an animal up': new day, new food – until one day the animal is slaughtered. Right up to the day before Thanksgiving, these patterns look the same. If you don't know the motivation of the pattern, why it is the way it is, you can't tell which pattern you are experiencing.

The regularities in the universe follow patterns, but like the turkey, we don't know which ones they are following. That is because as Hume argues previously, we don't have any experience of causality. That is why Hume says we have "suspicion that the course of nature may change." We would need some independent reason to think that the future will continue to be like the past – but that's exactly what we are missing. No amount of experimentation, or induction, will help us to answer Hume's riddle. And so we arrive at Hume's conclusion:

> **Conclusion:** Let the course of things be allowed hitherto ever so regular; that alone, without some new argument or inference, proves not that, for the future, it will continue so.

Hume knows that he is saying something extraordinary, so he goes on to spell out the consequences of what he has said. Sometimes this is worth doing. Your conclusion may be clear, but there is a risk that your reader may not fully appreciate its weight.

> **Consequences of conclusion spelled out:** In vain do you pretend to have learned the nature of bodies from your past experience. Their secret nature, and consequently all their effects and

influence, may change, without any change in their sensible qualities. This happens sometimes, and with regard to some objects; why may it not happen always, and with regard to all objects? What logic, what process of argument secures you against this supposition?

If we don't know the secret nature of things, we really don't know anything for certain. We don't know whether we should eat or breathe or sleep. Maybe the universe is just fattening us up, like the turkey, and maybe tomorrow is Thanksgiving.

CONSIDERING OBJECTIONS

Philosophy happens in dialogue. When you present an idea, other philosophers will raise objections, so when you are writing or presenting an idea in philosophy, you should put yourself in the role of the objector and try to find the strongest objections you can and answer them in advance. In the closing sentences of this paragraph, Hume does exactly that.

Objection 1: My practice, you say, refutes my doubts.

Hume is anticipating one of the oldest objections presented to sceptics, which is that no one can live as a sceptic. Hume liked a good meal, and used to strategically drop in on his friends in time for dinner. But if you really don't know if food will poison you, why eat it? If the past isn't a good guide for the future, why think there will be dinner later on? If Hume is such a sceptic, why do anything, why plan anything at all? It's a very good question. This brings us to a sixth rule of philosophical writing:

RULE 6: FIND THE BEST OBJECTIONS TO YOUR ARGUMENT AND ANSWER THEM.

Hume shows that he has thought about the objection, and points out that there is room for a distinction between the way we live and what we believe about the world.

> **Distinction:** But you mistake the purport of my question. As an agent, I am quite satisfied in the point; but as a philosopher, who has some share of curiosity, I will not say scepticism, I want to learn the foundation of this inference. No reading, no enquiry has yet been able to remove my difficulty, or give me satisfaction in a matter of such importance. Can I do better than propose the difficulty to the public, even though, perhaps, I have small hopes of obtaining a solution? We shall at least, by this means, be sensible of our ignorance, if we do not augment our knowledge.

Hume is pointing out an ambiguity in the objection that he does not act like a sceptic. The distinction is between Hume the agent and Hume the philosopher. Our last rule from Hume, then, is:

Rule 7: When something is ambiguous, introduce a distinction.

To see what Hume means, ask yourself this. Are you certain that your mother loves you? Most people would say yes. But does that mean that you have ruled out the possibility that your whole life is a cruel and complicated joke at your expense, perpetrated for unknown reasons, so that all your supposed friends and family are hired actors who mock you as soon as you are out of the room? It's hard to rule out this bizarre thought. But the funny thing is, even if it is hard to rule out, it doesn't alter the certainty that your mother loves you. Maybe the reason is that, like Hume, you make a distinction between yourself as an agent, a taker-of-actions who lives in the world and is loved by a mother, and yourself the philosopher, who entertains strange sceptical questions. Hume agrees that Hume the philosopher shouldn't know what to do. But it's not Hume the philosopher who shows up to dinner, it's Hume the agent.

Lessons in Reasoning

In this chapter, we unwound a single paragraph of Hume's. This is the best way to engage with philosophy, carefully considering why a philosopher says what he says. If you find that you read philosophy much more slowly than you would read something else, that is a sign that you are approaching philosophy in the right way.

Pausing to consider every step of a great philosopher's argument lets you feel the power of his reasoning. Once you've embarked with Hume you find yourself swept along to his sceptical conclusion. And yet, there is nothing in Hume that would have been surprising to the other empiricists, John Locke (1632 – 1704), George Berkeley (1685 – 1753), or indeed to most philosophers. Locke and Berkeley both did not reach Hume's level of scepticism, because they argued that an experience of causality is possible after all. Now that you understand Hume's argument, perhaps you too like Hume will be compelled to scepticism. Or perhaps you will adjust your philosophical compass to be more aligned with Locke or Berkeley or someone else, and try the argument again.

George Orwell's supremely helpful essay, "Politics and the English Language" offers six simple rules for writing better English. Orwell will teach you to write well. His rules are:

> NEVER USE A METAPHOR, SIMILE, OR OTHER FIGURE OF SPEECH WHICH YOU ARE USED TO SEEING IN PRINT.

> NEVER USE A LONG WORD WHERE A SHORT ONE WILL DO.

IF IT IS POSSIBLE TO CUT A WORD OUT, ALWAYS CUT IT OUT.

NEVER USE THE PASSIVE WHERE YOU CAN USE THE ACTIVE.

NEVER USE A FOREIGN PHRASE, A SCIENTIFIC WORD, OR A JARGON WORD IF YOU CAN THINK OF AN EVERYDAY ENGLISH EQUIVALENT.

BREAK ANY OF THESE RULES SOONER THAN SAY ANYTHING OUTRIGHT BARBAROUS.

Orwell's rules will help to make you a better writer in any field. As we discussed, a philosopher does not have to be a good writer, though as Hume shows us, he can be. If you want to write philosophy well, you will also need the seven rules we found in Hume.

BREAK LARGE, COMPLEX PROBLEMS INTO SMALLER, SIMPLER ONES.

CLEARLY EXPRESS A THESIS *UP FRONT*.

WHENEVER SOMETHING IS COMPLICATED OR ABSTRACT, GIVE AN EXAMPLE.

FRAME YOUR QUESTION OR TOPIC SO YOUR ARGUMENTS WILL SUPPORT YOUR THESIS.

MAKE YOUR ARGUMENT VALID AND SOUND.

FIND THE BEST OBJECTIONS TO YOUR ARGUMENT AND ANSWER THEM.

WHEN SOMETHING IS AMBIGUOUS, INTRODUCE A DISTINCTION.

A historian once told me that when he was given an exam as a PhD student, he was surprised to find that the questions were familiar. He had already answered them all in his very first exam as an undergraduate.

"Naturally," his supervisor told him, "The questions are the same. It is your answers that I expect to change."

I think Orwell had something similar in mind when he wrote that his rules of English writing seem simple but will transform your attitude if you put them into practice. The rules we have found in Hume are similar. They are simple enough to learn in a moment, but they will continue to improve your philosophical expression over the course of a lifelong friendship with wisdom.

5 – HOW PHILOSOPHY IS WRITTEN

SHOULD YOU WRITE?

SOME REASONS FOR WRITING

This chapter is about the different ways in which philosophy is written. If you are thinking about reading some philosophy, you may learn something about the structure of different philosophical types of writing. And if you are thinking about writing philosophy, then it is even more important to know the different ways in which philosophy is written.

But if you are going to write philosophy, the first question to ask yourself is *why?* What are you trying to accomplish?

Some philosophers have gotten the idea that they have to write in order to prove that they are real philosophers. This is false. Socrates (399 – 469 BC), the father of philosophy, wrote nothing at all. Since then many other philosophers have followed his example. This belief that you have to write in order to be a real philosopher confuses a sign for the thing signified. Philosophy is, as I have argued in my first chapter, a friendship with wisdom. If you can be bothered to write at length about philosophy, you probably do have a friendship with wisdom. But in the same way that going fishing is *a* sign but not the only sign of friendship, writing is only one of many signs that a friendship with wisdom exists.

"No man but a blockhead ever wrote, except for money", or so thought Samuel Johnson. Unfortunately there is very little money in philosophical writing. Philosophers who grow rich generally follow the example of Thales of Miletus (6th century BC) and apply their philosophical abilities to other fields. You will find philosophers in almost every field of endeavour: journalism, the stock market, consulting, the church, and all manner of white-collar work. You will also find philosophers who work with their hands, though in my experience there are fewer of these, perhaps because philosophical skill is harder to translate into that kind of work. Few of them are being paid for their writing about philosophy. And although university professors are paid to be philosophers, that is a salary. Academic writing is part of what you do to earn that salary: you're expected to publish books and articles. The articles themselves pay nothing at all, and books generally don't pay more than a few hundred dollars per year.

A much better reason for writing is to expose your way of thinking to the world. It is thrilling to see your ideas in print, and it's nice when others mention you in a way that proves they have read (or at least skimmed) your work. But here too caution is in order, and you should be prepared for a letdown. Every author privately imagines that his audience will rise as one to applaud him and say that they are persuaded forever. We imagine this, even though we ourselves have read many things and have never reacted in this way. Your audience will not react this way either – they may indeed be critical. For this reason, authors need to have thick skins. The real compliment paid to your work will be given unawares, when someone tells you what you had argued as though it was self-evident and he had always believed it.

Writing will also help to clarify your own ideas. Putting your ideas into written words forces you to organize them and show how they fit together. In this way, writing can be like teaching: the best way to understand something is often to explain it to somebody else.

If you do pick up writing as a habit I think you will encounter another reason for writing, which is that writing is a source of pleasure. People who are just beginning to write sometimes worry that they will run out of ideas. But once translating an idea into your authorial voice has become a habit, you find that interesting ideas are always floating up into view like sparks from a campfire. I like to take my time and choose an idea that I know I will enjoy thinking about, perhaps jotting down a few notes but mostly mulling it over at work and while doing chores. I like to wait for days or weeks until the need to write becomes a kind of pressure, and it is a joy to sit down at the keyboard and turn out a first draft.

Let's take stock. Writing does not pay well and does not guarantee much recognition. The only outcomes you can really count on are ones that come from you: clarifying ideas and enjoying an experience that is difficult to explain to those who do not write. I think perhaps this is why even the great philosopher Michel de Montaigne (1533 – 1592) humbly said that his friends were his audience. Or, as my grandfather, who made his living as an author, used to lament, writing makes a better mistress than a wife.

If you are setting out to write, you will need to follow the seven rules of writing that we learned from Hume in the previous chapter. But beyond that, you will need to ask yourself how big a project you have taken on. Is it big enough to occupy a whole book? Can you get through it in an article? Is it counterintuitive enough that you want to lead your audience to it slowly, through a dialogue? Do you have a cluster of atomic, aphoristic ideas? The answer will help to determine what kind of thing you produce.

And if you are not planning to write, you'll still gain something out of considering the different forms of philosophical writing from a writer's point of view. Reading a dialogue is not like reading an essay, and an essay is not like a set of fragments. It's easier to see what the author meant if you understand some of his constraints.

Let us begin where the vast majority of philosophical works are published today, in academia.

ACADEMIC WRITING

PUBLISH OR PERISH

If you want to understand academic publishing, it helps to understand Goodhart's law. Suppose the boss wants to be sure his factories are doing well, so he begins to hand out bonuses based on how many units each factory has produced. You can bet that all factories will devote their energies to producing more units. Soon a larger quantity of units will be produced, but the quality of the units will be lower than it was before since everyone is now trying to produce as many as possible. Perhaps raw materials will be squandered for the sake of an increase in production. In the end, the boss may end up losing money even with all the additional units, because of the cost of refunds and wasted raw materials. In this story, the boss has encountered Goodhart's law: when a metric is established, it is instantly gamed and ceases to have meaning. In academia, as they say, you must publish or perish. Publications are a metric, and the metric is constantly being gamed.

Within living memory, one could hear respected scholars talk about "my article", meaning the one article published to cap a long career of teaching and research. But over the course of the last century, hiring and promotion became tied to publication, and universities began to focus on the number of publications a scholar had. This led clever academics to stretch out their ideas to write as much as possible. An idea that would once have been put into a footnote is now expanded into a journal article. Much academic writing has become tedious and unpleasant to read, but no one is measuring whether the writing is good, only whether it is plentiful.

The problem is that not only academics, but the institutions that employ them have fallen victim to Goodhart's law.

Universities are funded by student tuition and donations from former students, but they also depend on government grants and funding. One of the ways in which universities make themselves more prestigious, and thus more eligible for all the sources of money just mentioned, is to have their own university press. For this reason, even small schools usually have a publishing imprint. They sell very few books to libraries and often operate at a loss, but that's OK. The university profits because prestige is profitable, and academics profit because publishing books is tied to hiring and promotion.

The same used to be true of academic journals, which began as small projects owned and operated by philosophy departments to publish brief reflections on the discipline. However, in the second half of the last century, profiteers swept into the academic publishing market and greatly expanded it, recognizing the potential for exploiting Goodhart's law in a system that would not self-correct. They bought up academic journals, packaged them together, and then raised the price of a subscription to thousands or tens of thousands of dollars per year. They also seeded new journals, creating new income streams. They knew that academics have to publish, and university libraries have to buy what is published. Taken as a whole, the parasitic journal industry that they created is worth billions of dollars per year.

The result is that journals have become a perverse system in which universities pay many times for the same content. A scholar, who is being paid by a university, writes an article, and submits it, for free, to a journal. The article is reviewed by an editor, who may receive an honorarium of a few thousand dollars per year, but nothing near the value of the time he devotes to the journal. He has this time to give because he works for a university too. The editor sends the article to two or three peer reviewers who review it for nothing, and who usually work at universities as well. They and the editor correct the article and prepare it for publication. The article then is published, which is to say it appears on the journal website behind a paywall and in some cases also in a print version. The journal may contribute by formatting the article. By publishing, the author releases his rights to the journal. The publisher then sells the product back to the institutions that employ the scholar, the editor and the peer reviewers. Many journals no longer provide even the author with a print or digital copy. If you want to quote your own article correctly, with the proper page numbers, you can pay like everyone else.

When a factory owner discovers Goodhart's law and realizes his metrics are losing him money, he can try something else. Why, you might be wondering, has that not happened at the university? The answer is that the costs are borne by people who can't do much about it: students (or their parents) who pay tuition, donors, and taxpayers. Nobody really likes academic publishing, but everyone is tied into it. There have been some attempts to start new, open access journals to avoid what they see as the corruption of the publishing industry. The trouble is that because these journals are new, they are not very prestigious. You will have to decide for yourself whether it is worth going through the trouble of getting an academic publication, only to end up at the bottom of the totem pole in an open access journal.

PEER REVIEW

The process that supposedly confers a special legitimacy on academic writing is peer review. Peer review is a mechanism whereby most articles and books must be considered by two or three peers, that is, two or three scholars with knowledge of the area. As a rule, the editor will take a look at submissions he receives, and may discard those that are completely hopeless, not even close to the right format, or just crazy. However, most authors are writing as experts, and the editor may not share their expertise. For example, the editor of a journal on ancient philosophy may be an Aristotle (384 – 322 BC) scholar and not up to date on the latest material on Epicurus (341 – 270 BC). So the editor will send your article or book to people who do know that area. The editor selects these scholars and invites them to review your article. Peer review is blind: they don't know who you are, and you can't find out who they are. However, if their comments are detailed, the editor will usually share them with you.

At its best, peer review means that even if your article or book is rejected, you will receive two or three anonymous but expert sets of comments and questions which will recognize what is good in your work and show you where to improve: a home inspector's report on the state of your philosophical architecture. Along with the referee's comments comes a recommendation, either to publish, to publish with certain necessary changes, to "revise and resubmit", or a no. In order to get published, all the peer reviewers must agree. Revise and resubmit often puzzles new writers. It means that the journal thinks there may be value in your ideas, but that the draft is unpublishable as is. It's an invitation to revisit everything and then consider resubmission to the same journal, so that the process can begin again. Even if you do revise and resubmit, acceptance is not guaranteed.

At its worst, peer review is useless and nasty for all the same reasons that nastiness emerges among anonymous commenters on the internet. Comments can be petty and insulting. It sometimes seems as if reviewers are wilfully misunderstanding what you are saying.

Peer review also functions to reinforce orthodoxy. In some ways this is a good thing. If an idea is completely new to you, odds are that there is a reason why it isn't already in the canon. A conservative reflex in scholarship can be a good thing, but it also stifles the sort of creative approach to philosophy that used to be common. Toward the middle of the last century, articles were often quite wide-ranging. Today the careful writer keeps his points narrow, because if you try to make too many points you risk spooking one of your reviewers and then your whole article is turned down. Better for everyone to expand your thinking over multiple articles and books: after all, you must publish or perish.

Peer review also creates an incentive for critical (but not too critical) engagement with as much as possible of what has been published on your subject, even if much of it is not really worth mentioning. Perhaps Jones has published a particularly incoherent book on your subject. When teaching or thinking about the matter, you pay absolutely no attention to Jones. But when you write your article, your reviewer might wonder why Jones is not mentioned. Are you unaware of Jones' work? The peer reviewer is going to add, "Should address the work of Jones." Or, horror of horrors, the peer reviewer might *be* Jones. He's going to turn down your article, since it doesn't address what he thinks is the most important work on the subject: his. To prevent this, authors often write a long 'literature review' in which they try to namedrop everything that matters. In most modern articles, you can flip through the literature review to get to the actual thesis without missing much.

When your piece is accepted, it will usually be "accepted with changes". This means that the editor will want to change a few things. For example, he may alter your citations to fit the house style. But there may be big changes as well. At this point, you are negotiating. You can reject some changes and try to arrive at a final product. I once published a piece where the editor wanted to change my references from B.C., Before Christ, to the absurd B.C.E., Before the 'Common Era', an era that apparently begins with the birth of Jesus Christ but somehow cannot make reference to this fact. I said I was willing to withdraw my piece over this, and it was duly published with B.C. Your own stubbornness must dictate your choices here.

ACADEMIC ARTICLES

Most of what professional philosophers publish today are articles. These appear in academic journals or books of conference proceedings or collections of papers by known authors on particular subjects, and run from around 5 to 50 pages in length. Some journals take a general approach to philosophy but most specialize, by area (for example, ancient philosophy), method (for example, philosophy in the analytic method), or approach (for example, only well-written and literary philosophical articles). If you are looking to pad an academic CV, some journals are better than others. As a rule, the better a journal is, the more exclusive it is, and exclusivity is measured by the percentage of submissions that are rejected. Good journals will reject well over ninety percent of what they receive.

If you read articles from the earlier part of the last century, you will find that they vary quite a bit in the way they are constructed. The pressure to publish and the effect of peer review has narrowed academic publishing so that most articles now have the same basic structure:

(1) Literature review

(2) The main point

(3) Consideration of objections

(4) Concluding section

You'll see this structure repeated again and again. In part that's because it is also a method for stretching short points into long articles, since there is always plenty to say about what other people have already written. Even if your main point is very modest, you can easily pad it out with objections. Though most people do follow this four point formula, there's no rule that says you must write this way, and you will find exceptional articles that are differently structured and still passed peer review.

As the reader of an academic article, you can use the structure to your advantage. One way to read an article is to flip through the literature review section to get to the main point the author is trying to argue.

But you can also use articles for the literature review sections. Something written recently is likely to tell you who else you need to read to gain an understanding of the area.

If you do write for a journal, pick up a copy of the journal (go to a library, or search creatively online) and see how articles are formatted. Your article should look more or less like that. Journals or their websites will usually tell you how to submit an article, but the basic process is to send it *via* email or, more and more frequently, through a website portal. If you do send a covering email, keep it short. You don't need to tell the editor much about you, just the name of your article, a brief (e.g. two sentences) summary of what you're trying to show, and your contact information. Expect peer review to take months, in some cases it can drag on for around a year. In a couple of months if you have heard nothing, you can safely write back to ask for an update. You are not supposed to shop your article around to multiple journals simultaneously.

When you do get your comments back, it can be disheartening to read them. It can seem as though your article has been torn to shreds. One of the best pieces of advice I ever received was from the mail-in era: when you send an article, put a second copy in an envelope addressed to your second choice journal. The reason that this is good advice is that it is very easy to abandon hope the first time you are rejected. If you sit on a rejection for more than 24 hours, you probably won't send the article out again. So don't wait. When I make a submission, even though I don't have envelopes at the ready, I think about my first and my next choice of journal. That way, if I get back anything but an acceptance or a revise-and-resubmit, it's just a matter of incorporating anything of value in the comments and sending it off to the next place within a day.

ACADEMIC BOOKS

Academic books tend to have the same structure as academic articles, but the structure is sometimes stretched over the length of the book, and at other times repeated in each chapter. Just as with academic articles you have to choose a journal, if you are writing a book you need to choose your press. Most universities have their own presses. Some specialize, and most are slightly more open to publishing their own alumni. And as journals do with article submissions, presses will also send your book manuscript out for peer review. Your book will either be rejected or accepted, probably with some mandated changes. You and the editor will have to come to an agreement on a final product.

If you compare a book written in the last century to one written today, you will probably find that the newer book has a narrower scope. This is the result of market saturation. There are so many academics who have very narrow specializations that showing the breadth of knowledge once considered scholarly means that you are stepping into the areas of expertise of lots of other people. All these other people will raise tiny but implacable objections against you. Narrowing your scope makes it easier to get published.

One of the tricks that one learns in the academy is how to approach a book, which is to say, how to do the pre-research that will make it much easier to read an academic book and indeed to decide whether that book is worth reading. You can read the blurb on the back or on the publisher's website, of course. Another option is to flip through the table of contents. Academic books usually use the table of contents to say exactly what they are going to be about. If you have the book handy, you can flip through the introduction. It's conventional to end one's introduction with a brief summary of every chapter.

Most useful of all, there are book reviews. When an academic book is published, academics review it for journals. These reviews are then published. A review is not very prestigious, and it doesn't count for much on your CV. It does, however, let you have your say about a particular work. A good reviewer begins by explaining what the book is about, and then raising problems or questions that seem to him to be left over. If you are trying to decode a particularly tricky piece of academic writing, reviews can be extremely helpful.

And then there is the bibliography. A bibliography is supposed to be a guide to the books you drew on to write your book, but most scholars also use the bibliography to show off their knowledge of an area and prove that they haven't left anything out. For the reader, this is a snapshot of everything else in the area at the time of publication. If you are trying to extend your mental map of a particular area of philosophy, there is little more useful than a well written bibliography.

ACADEMIC ENCYCLOPEDIAS

Even fifty years ago, someone wanting a quick overview of a topic or area in philosophy needed to buy a small dictionary of philosophy, slog through the dreariness of a textbook, or trudge over to a library to look things up. The internet has changed this for the better. It is now very easy to find out the state of the art on a particular topic by looking it up in an online encyclopedia. The most reliable of these is the Stanford Encyclopedia of Philosophy (SEP), which is regularly edited and updated by people familiar with the state of the art. It will therefore tell you what everyone who is actively working on a particular area of philosophy thinks. The bibliography section is quite valuable as well. Of course, being up to date on what the academy thinks means that the SEP will contain a full-strength dose of whatever political correctness currently grips the academy. In such cases, the bibliography, at least, should point you toward something less shrill.

POLITICAL BIAS IN ACADEMIC WRITING

Although universities are not inherently partisan, the vast majority of philosophy professors are on the Left, and you will find that reflected in their writings. This is an open secret among academics. If you are on the Left, academia welcomes you. If not, it is good to remember that like many people who live in monocultures, academics greatly overestimate their own open-mindedness toward views they do not share.

In metaphysics or epistemology, you'll only notice this in illustrations and the affectation of using "she" as the indefinite pronoun. In politics or ethics, you'll find certain assumptions taken for granted, for example that hierarchies are wicked, and that the pre-modern world was too unforgiving, especially of the sexual foibles of its inhabitants. You'll also find anyone who transgresses against the taboos of our time, including virtually every great philosopher, dismissed as a bigot. At times this can be difficult to endure, and you must see for yourself how much of such silliness you can stomach. I read academic books for their specialized content, but otherwise I'd generally prefer something non-academic or written before 1970.

FOR-PROFIT WRITING

ARTICLES

Outside the realm of professional philosophy, there are a lot of magazines that touch on philosophy. Some are about philosophy, but presented in such a way as to be accessible to the non-specialist. Some are about philosophy and something else, often philosophy and politics or philosophy and religion.

Submitting an article for publication is a much simpler process with regular magazines than with academic journals. As with a journal, you will need to do a bit of digging to find out where to submit your article. Submission will probably be through email. Don't overthink the covering email: explain that this is an original piece written by you, give your title, and a brief (one to two sentences) description of what you're saying.

Magazines are usually faster at responding than journals are. Even for a top magazine, you generally only need to wait for a month to inquire what has become of your article. (And, especially for magazines, don't be shy: editors are very busy and often misplace or forget about articles, so they can use the reminder.) Your article won't go through peer review, though the editor may work with you to round off some rough edges. If the editor demands you add or remove something and you don't want to do it, you can always withdraw your article. But don't be too quick to withdraw it: the role of editors is rarely acknowledged, but theirs is a real skill. Even though no one likes to be edited, they may well make your work better.

Although I've included magazines under for-profit writing, the profit is not guaranteed and it is seldom generous. Within living memory, one could expect a hefty payout from placing an article in a big magazine. Today it is still possible to get paid, and some writers do. But most magazines are barely holding it together financially, and they will pay you occasionally, or slowly, or not at all. Even though they don't pay, they get plenty of submissions. So unfortunately, as a writer of articles, you are competing with people willing to give their work away for free.

Despite all this, publishing in magazines can be a very good experience. Magazines bring a certain level of exposure. It's likely that your friends read the magazines that you read, and so writing for a magazine comes closest to Michel de Montaigne's (1533 – 1592) ideal of writing for one's friends. It is a way to put your writing out there, to make your view available and to contribute, in some fashion, to the grand conversation.

BOOKS

Non-academic books, like magazine articles, pass through an editing process, but they are generally not subject to peer review. Partly for this reason, such books do not count (or at least not much) as academic publications. This means that when writing a non-academic book, there is always the implicit question, why not present your findings to the specialists? Are you afraid that your findings won't hold up? The costs and the implicit challenge mean that very few academics publish for-profit books. But when they do, they have chosen freedom over restriction, and so for-profit books in philosophy are often broader and more interesting than academic books. You won't be sorry, for example, if you pick up any of the non-academic books of David Stove (1927 – 1994) or Sir Roger Scruton (1944 – 2020).

If you decide to write a non-academic book in philosophy, it should be clear and easy to understand. Much of your audience will be encountering your topic for the first time. It is also a good idea to write in self-contained sections, for your audience may be busy, and may pick your book up, read for a little while, attend to something else, and then return to the book again.

Usually if your book is accepted by a non-academic publisher, the publisher thinks he can make some money on it. Even for-profit writing is not very lucrative, but your publisher will try to advertise and then sell your book (as much as he is able). Until not so long ago, your only real options to publish were books and articles. The situation has been completely upended by the internet.

THE INTERNET

VANITY PRESSES AND PUBLISHING ONLINE

Before the internet, there were companies that everyone called vanity presses. They tried to look like publishing houses and had a legitimate-looking logo that they put on books, but they would print anything, no matter how awful, so long as you paid for the print run. Vanity presses existed to allow people to pretend that they had published a book, and then inflict it on friends and family at Christmas.

That's how it used to be. But even before the internet changed publishing, clever authors had started to use vanity presses in a different way. By the late 90s and early 2000s there were so many presses that it was getting harder to recognize when a book came from a vanity press. One scholar I know wrote a book of which he knew he could sell many copies at speaking engagements. He realized it would be cheaper to print it himself with a vanity press and then keep all the profits when he sold a copy, so that was what he did. The internet has made such schemes easier and even less expensive.

Today, much of the really bad writing that used to be put into vanity presses is found in blogs and self-published e-books. But along with it, many talented authors have taken advantage of digital publishing. They recognize that publishing does not provide what it used to. For the main thing that publishers used to provide was exclusive access to technology for distributing the written word: a printing press. Today your book can be exclusively an e-book, or you can print it *via* a print-on-demand service. Publishing houses today are getting by on the secondary value that they provide, by offering nice formatting, cover design and publicity. These are good things, but they will cost you a percentage of your book sales. No wonder that many authors are choosing to publish their own books.

BLOGS

If you want to write regularly without going through the trouble of submission and editing by a journal or a magazine, you can always blog. There is no bar for entry: a blog can be set up for free or at little cost. If you are willing to pay a little more, you can have the satisfaction of tracking your audience, finding out where they are, what of yours they read, and for how long. Then it is up to you to populate your blog with insights that are good enough to build an audience, and regular enough to bring that audience back again.

Even though I have tried my hand at blogging, I continue to marvel at the existence of blogs. They are the total repudiation of Johnson's assertion that no reasonable person would write except for money. But that is how it is, and many clever and talented people are bloggers, some of them writing much more (though not, always, better) than even regular newspaper columnists used to do. To be fair, some bloggers do derive profit from their writing, and those who update regularly usually find a way to monetize their site through advertisements, product placement, or merchandising.

If you are thinking about blogging, it is worth considering a few points. First, there is the time commitment. Blogs need to be updated regularly or your audience will melt away. Those regular updates are like exercise: once you've missed one, it's difficult to get back into the routine. Regular updates mean regularly finding bloggable ideas. This means you'll need to be generating new and interesting ideas every day, or week, or month, depending on the schedule you set yourself. Generating these ideas is easiest if you are always thinking about philosophy and being stimulated by the ideas of others so that you can use them as jumping off points for your own. Being in or putting yourself in an environment conducive to such thoughts will help.

Another consideration in this time of reduced employee rights is whether you have the liberty to publish a blog. This is especially worth considering if your blog is going to veer into politics. Will employers or colleagues hold it against you? Will they possibly hold comments made by others but appearing on your blog against you? If you are concerned, you might consider blogging under a pen name.

Philosophy blogs can become online philosophy communities, led by the writer, and thriving in the comments section. If you are thinking about self-publishing in philosophy, blogs can also be ways to grow an audience who will buy your books.

From the point of view of a reader, blogs in philosophy can be good resources, especially if the blogger is exploring an area that's of interest to you. The quality of blogs will vary a great deal, however. The product is free, after all.

WRITTEN ARGUMENT ON THE INTERNET

Online resources like blogs, fora, chat rooms, and even email offer much opportunity for written philosophical argument. I have noticed that arguing about philosophy in this form tends to take on a specific shape, where each reply becomes longer than the one before it, and the argument finally ends in exhaustion. The shape isn't particular to online exchanges; the correspondence networks of the 18th century often led to a similar outcome. When René Descartes (1596 – 1650) published his *Meditations on First Philosophy*, he sent it around for comments from some of the greatest philosophers of his time. The *Meditations* are short, punchy and persuasive. The objections that Descartes received were long and cautious. Descartes considered their objections and wrote replies, also at length. The collected *Objections and Replies* are much, much longer than the *Meditations*. I have never been able to read the *Objections and Replies* without a sense of sadness at the way they mar the beauty and clarity of the *Meditations*, which, after all, is a work that speaks for itself, and doesn't need Descartes' attempts at restating what he has already said.

When an argument is conducted in writing, it tends to take on the expanding structure of the *Objections and Replies*. An author briefly states a point. An objector raises an objection which explains the point and then the objection. The original author offers a longer reply reframing the objection and explaining why the objection does not work. The objector explains why this reframing is wrong and spells out a different way in which the objection can work. Soon, very soon, the argument is longer than the original piece, which turns out to be like the point of a pyramid, supported by an ever growing base of philosophical argument.

The pyramid shape is caused as the author and the objector both retreat into their more general assumptions. When those are challenged, both retreat to the assumptions which ground them. These sorts of exchanges can be helpful if you are trying to understand the points of view of the interlocutors. Some people enjoy them, and if you do, many resources are available to you.

For my own part, I much prefer in-person dialogue. It's easier to follow the point and not get bogged down in founding assumptions. I suspect that is why Plato (429 – 347 BC) and Aristotle (384 – 322 BC) considered dialogue, and not writing, to be the fundamental mode of philosophy.

TRADITIONAL PHILOSOPHICAL FORMS

DIALOGUES

I've lost count of how many times students and friends have complained to me that they aren't allowed to write dialogues. Plato (429 – 347 BC) wrote dialogues, after all, and what could be more authentic than to write as he wrote? In fact, there is still a market for dialogues, which can be published in magazines if they are short enough, and in books if they are longer. But most people who actually do write a dialogue soon learn two things. First, dialogues are not easy to write. And secondly, dialogues are more open to interpretation than other forms of philosophical writing. The characters in your dialogues will not stay where you put them but will take on lives and meanings of their own.

Dialogues are hard to write because in the dialogue form, you are artfully walking the reader toward your thesis. Now, chances are you made several false starts as you were trying to work out your view. Are your characters going to explore all these ultimately bad directions before they go in the direction you went? If so, your characters will be more psychologically realistic, but your dialogue will be longer and more rambling. What is more, you may find that you didn't have good reasons for abandoning a line of inquiry, you just abandoned it. But when you make a character do that, your reader will find it unsatisfying. But suppose to avoid this you decide to tighten up the dialogue and get rid of the false starts. Your characters will make a bee-line for your thesis. The clearer you make your dialogue, the more your main character surges toward your view and the other characters just wave him through, the more the reader wonders why you didn't just write an article or a book. When you write a dialogue, you are confronted with the same problems that confront a novelist or a dramatist. Your characters must be real enough that the reader can identify with them to some extent. You have to capture enough of the messiness of the world to create a kind of vivarium in which your characters can move about, but not so much that it detracts from what they have to say. And you have to master the art of pacing your argument, moving through it not too slowly or quickly, but just at the speed that your reader requires. None of these are easy skills to master, but some philosophers do master them. That is when they encounter the second problem with dialogues.

A friend of mine once wrote and published an excellent dialogue. I read it several times, both as a draft and after it appeared in a magazine. But each time it seemed to me to end in uncertainty, on a question, like an early Socratic dialogue. In fact, that was one of the things I liked most about it. But my friend, the author, had not intended it to be open-ended. It seemed to him that the dialogue suggested a single conclusion, one which he found obvious, and it annoyed him that no one else seemed to find it as obvious as he did. His characters had taken on lives of their own, but it wasn't the life he had tried to breathe into them. And so what seemed to me to be an excellent piece came to disappoint him, and he never published any of the other dialogues he had planned.

Every philosopher loves the dialogues of Plato. But I often wonder whether Plato, if he could see the reception of his dialogues across history, would be as bitter as my friend. Even in antiquity, there was great disagreement about what you were supposed to get out of Plato's dialogues, and the very different schools that we now call Sceptics and Neoplatonists both claimed to be following Plato's lead.

When you are reading historical dialogues, like the dialogues of Plato, you are on the other side of this problem. You are trying to find out what the dialogue is about. One way to quickly orient yourself in a dialogue is to find the author's mouthpiece: the character through which the author's views are being laid out. But it is not even always obvious which character serves as the mouthpiece for the philosopher's own views. Plato – at least in his early and middle dialogues – makes it easy to see who speaks for him: it is Socrates. But other dialogues are not so clear. In George Berkeley's (1685 – 1753) dialogue, *Alciphron*, Berkeley makes two different characters speak for him. And readers still argue over which character represents the author in David Hume's (1711 – 1776) *Dialogues Concerning Natural Religion*. One of the characters *resembles* Hume, but the narrator of the dialogue attributes victory to a different character. Is this an unreliable narrator? Or was Hume himself more uncertain than later philosophers have supposed? Is the dialogue supposed to have many winners? It is difficult to know.

APHORISMS

Some writers have the knack of capturing a philosophical thought in a single clear observation: an aphorism. Friederich Nietzsche (1844 – 1900), for example, was a talented aphorist. Here is one of his: "It is the privilege of greatness to grant supreme pleasure through trifling gifts." (*Human, All Too Human*, translated by Helen Zimmern Section 9, 496). Nietzsche's observation helps to explain the delight that a sports fan feels at receiving a scuffed and used ball or a sweaty shirt from an athlete. The observation might be expanded to explain many other things: the enduring interest in the doings of the House of Windsor, the relics of Saints, the preference for autographed books.

Digging meaning out of an aphorism is your job as the reader – and this job puts some demands on you. You get no introduction and no conclusion, you have to do the work of figuring out how the aphorism maps onto the world. Human beings are predisposed to see patterns, to abstract figure from ground. The same skill which, perhaps, enabled our ancestors to spot camouflaged animals moving through the grass makes us see shapes in the clouds and faces in burnt toast. At their best, aphorisms activate this search for meaning and point us toward a truth that is worth discerning. When an aphorism falls flat, there's not enough there to get you started.

Once you have thought through the implications of an aphorism, well then it's on to the next aphorism, and the process begins again. Again you have to supply the framing and dig out the hidden meaning. Some of us find the process of reading aphorisms tiring.

Just as some people hanker after writing dialogues, some wish they could write aphorisms. And as with dialogues, nothing really stands in your way, except for the task of finding someone to read or publish your aphorisms. Since your reader needs to do so much more of the work, your reader needs some reason to think he can trust that you are saying something of value in the first place. In the past, aphorisms were usually written by those who had already established a reputation in some other way.

FRAGMENTS

Along with the belief that ancient statues were unpainted white marble, another great misconception about the ancient world is that ancient philosophers wrote aphorisms. They didn't. Ancient philosophers wrote poems, dialogues and books. Heraclitus (around the 6th century BC) is famous for observing that "you cannot step into the same river twice". Protagoras (around 485 –415 BC) is famous for claiming that "man is the measure of all things". Like aphorisms, these short statements are deeply suggestive of a more developed philosophical account. But unlike aphorisms, they were never intended to stand alone, for these are fragments.

Fragments are sometimes literal fragments: scraps of papyrus that were once part of a book of philosophy discovered in an ancient garbage dump or entombed in a city buried by a volcano. But for the most part, fragments are quotations in other works, works that have survived. Fortunately for us, it was conventional in antiquity to quote at length.

Our knowledge of many ancient authors comes entirely from the way they were quoted in antiquity. As a result, our encounters with them are framed by others who chose to quote them, often centuries later, and often with their own authorial agendas. German classicists of the 19th century produced books of fragments, identifying fragments across more than a thousand years of literature and organizing them by author. Taking a scholarly approach to fragments means trying to use the tiny clues of context to imaginatively reconstruct the larger works of which they are tiny parts.

In a strange way, fragments have come to be appreciated as if they were aphorisms, in much the same way that the faded statues of antiquity generated a new art form, the unpainted marble statue. It is possible to take Heraclitus' or Protagoras' fragments as the starting point for further reflection, even if these reflections do not go where the author intended. Perhaps this shows that even those who do not write dialogues take the risk that a tiny piece of their works might one day take on an independent and unexpected life of its own.

ESSAYS

Almost everyone has written an essay or two at school. It is a form of writing that was invented by the philosopher Michel de Montaigne (1533 – 1592), and he put his guiding principle in the name. An essay is an attempt, a proposal, a foray into an interesting question. The casual approach reflects old world sophistication: the ideal essayist has read everything and gained a deep understanding of the area, but his product is not a plodding tome but something light and enjoyable. An essay is supposed to look like a chatty first draft that touches on many things and arrives, as if by accident, at a conclusion. It is the written equivalent of visiting a genteel scholar with a question. Instead of answering, he chats with you as you both wander through his cabinet of curiosities where he picks up items seemingly at random to explain them to you, each marvelous in its own way, until as you are leaving he says a few words that tie everything together and you recognize to your surprise that all along he has been assembling the pieces of an answer.

As is often true, in essay writing it takes a lot of work to make it look easy. It's even more difficult to write an essay that moves with apparent effortlessness while also constructing a philosophical account. The challenge of writing essays and the pleasure of reading them made the style popular in the centuries after Montaigne. That in turn made essays a kind of default assignment for schoolchildren. Unfortunately, this had the effect of leeching much of the fun out of form, as children and students ground out formulaic essays. In this way, the essay is just another casualty of the optimism of 19th century educators regarding what can be taught.

When reading an essay, you will generally have to trace the argument through its sections. The good news is that a well written essay is a pleasure to read, and so this task will not be burdensome. The bad news is that reading an essay is like watching a magic show. Sometimes you need to choose between being delighted by the art and understanding how the thing is done.

Many philosophers are happy to leave essays to their reluctant students. Very occasionally, philosophers publish an essay in a magazine, or collect their essays in a book. It's a shame, because the essay is a subtle tool, perhaps the only one subtle enough to portray the frailty and doubt, as well as the wonder, that characterizes a friendship with wisdom.

THE GEOMETRIC METHOD

The *Ethics* of Baruch Spinoza (1632 – 1677) is written in what Spinoza himself identified as the geometric method. The book begins with numbered definitions and axioms, and launches into numbered propositions, followed by proofs and corollaries. Each proof ends with a triumphant Q.E.D., short for *quod erat demonstrandum*, meaning, 'which was to be shown'. This means the proof has got to the proposition it was trying to establish.

Spinoza was consciously echoing the method used by actual geometers, for example Euclid (4th century BC) in his *Elements*. In this stylistic choice Spinoza was demonstrating the affinity many philosophers (and in particular Spinoza's contemporaries) felt for the methods and proofs of mathematics.

As a rule, philosophers number their paragraphs to indicate logical priority. The idea is that things that come earlier are broader, more likely to be obvious: axioms. Then the text builds to arrive at claims you may not have recognized were always implicit in what came before.

In the 20th century, philosophers following the analytic method once again became interested in mathematics, but in a different way. Some, like Ludwig Wittgenstein (1889 – 1951), once again wrote in numbered propositions, though for Wittgenstein it is not clear that the argument is unfurling in an attempt to achieve geometric clarity. For most analytic philosophers, the homage to mathematics was expressed by an attempt to bring language as close as possible to mathematics. Propositions and whole arguments were reduced to their structures, the semantic content slid (or shoehorned) into variables so that the reader could focus on the skeleton of logical relations. For many philosophers, this sort of analysis has become second nature, and in reading analytic philosophy you will find that arguments are often reduced to numbered variables with modifiers in numbered propositions.

If you are interested in philosophy, you will almost certainly feel the draw of mathematics. You may also find your own thoughts are clarified by setting them out in logical terms, so that you can clearly see the logical relations they bear to one another. But there are literary reasons, I think, not to follow the geometric method or rely very heavily on analysis, for both of these are ways of forcing your reader to spell out your argument with you. In this way, we might plot different types of philosophical writing on a spectrum. At one end are aphorisms and mathematized philosophy. These come to you in pieces, like IKEA furniture, with most of the assembly left to you. At the other end you find beautiful forms like essays and dialogues. We might compare these to beautiful handmade furniture, and perhaps like such furniture they are sometimes kept for the sake of beauty rather than function.

MEDIEVAL QUESTIONS

One way of organizing different modes of philosophical writing is to think of them as the expressions of a certain period of philosophy. Through no fault of the pre-Socratic philosophers, we encounter philosophy before Socrates (469 – 399 BC) almost entirely in the form of fragments. We encounter Socrates himself in dialogue, and the dialogue was widely used in antiquity. Aristotle's (384 – 322 BC) lost dialogues were said to rival even those of Plato (429 – 347 BC) in the beauty of their expression. We encounter the Hellenistic period largely in fragments. In the early modern period, we find the 17th century dominated by the geometric method, followed by the 18th century which was dominated by the essay.

I have, of course, left a large hole in my story, for the ancient world did not lead immediately into the modern one. But in order to approach philosophy of the middle ages, we need to know something about the specific forms of the medieval university. The period that hubristically called itself the Enlightenment called the middle ages the Dark Ages, and the term stuck. But the truth is stranger: as far as scholarship goes, the middle ages were remarkably similar to our own time. Then as now, most philosophy happened at the university, where it was conducted in a stylized format. The academic style ensured that scholars from different universities could easily understand one another's work. To outsiders, then as now, these forms were a barrier to understanding.

Today, for example, every person entitled to the degree of PhD, doctor of philosophy, has produced a final, stylized piece of student work: a dissertation, also called a PhD thesis. This is a piece of original research, produced under the watchful eye of several other scholars. In order to graduate, the PhD candidate must defend the thesis against these scholars, plus other examiners, to their satisfaction:

the questioners must rule that the defence was successful. As a consequence, dissertations are usually horrible to read, because they were written to satisfy a committee with different demands and opinions. Students often wonder at the number of plodding philosophical commentaries on the *Sentences* of the theologian Peter Lombard (1096 – 1160). The reason there are so many is that a commentary on the sentences played roughly the same role as a PhD dissertation today: it was a final project necessary to rise in the academic hierarchy.

Medieval scholars served their communities as knowledge hubs. If you had a question, you were entitled to go and ask a scholar. The scholars would answer in public, and these answers were often recorded for posterity. You could ask a medieval scholar questions about pretty much anything: from practical questions about what course of treatment you should undergo to theological questions such as whether an animal born with two heads has two souls. Students also asked questions. The process of answering questions became a mode of philosophy in its own right. We see it at its best in the most important work of the medieval period, St. Thomas Aquinas' (1225 – 1274) masterpiece, the *Summa Theologica*.

To read medieval questions, it helps to imaginatively enter the world of the medieval scholar. The question is asked. St. Thomas listens to the question. I imagine him nodding along, eyes closed as he allows the logic to spool out before his mind's eye. Others, perhaps students or even the questioner himself, jump in with suggestions. Some take a position which St. Thomas immediately recognizes as wrong. Others take a position based on the Christian or philosophical tradition which, while not wrong, St. Thomas sees is incomplete. He listens patiently as his razor intellect trims every excess from their arguments to preserve only the core. Finally, he answers. First, he restates all the suggestions he has heard, followed by the views that are not quite wrong but need to be set in context, so clearly that their authors nod along, satisfied with his characterization. Then he states his own position, beginning with the Latin word, *respondeo*, "I answer that...". Finally, he points out the flaw in each objection, and his responses are devastating. In the *Summa*, we find this drama encapsulated in each question. The reader may find himself in any of the views advanced. I often find myself in the initial objections, only to be bowled over by the strength of St. Thomas' answer. One way to enjoy medieval questions, then, is as a member of the audience: listening to the objections, contemplating some standard view, then hearing the subtle reply of the master. Another way to read medieval questions is to look for the master's view up front, then consider the objections if you are not convinced.

ON READING AND THE SHORTNESS OF LIFE

DON'T READ BAD BOOKS

When I was in graduate school, a few words from a wise professor changed my approach to philosophical reading and writing – and I would like to pass these words on to you. The professor had picked a brand new book by a famous philosopher as our reading for a course. The book was so new that we ordered it before it was printed, and got it just in time to begin. By the second chapter, it was clear that the book was a disappointment: it was boring, pedantic, bad. And then the professor said something I had never dared to think before: "Life is short. Let's not finish this book."

Up until then, up until that very moment, I think, I had prided myself on finishing every book I picked up. Suddenly it was clear to me how silly that was. I am not saying that you should only read books with which you already agree. But if a book is bloviating, annoyingly partisan, or just silly, that is a good reason for putting it down. If a book has a lot to say but then ends in a mealy-mouthed conclusion designed not to offend any peer-reviewer, that is a reason to put the book down after the good bits and not bother with the conclusion. You the reader have a limited amount of time and an almost unlimited supply of potential reading material. It makes sense to be choosy.

Some philosophers worry that if they only read books that are well written, they will miss out on something very important but ill expressed, the proverbial diamond in the rough. We might call this worry the *diamond in the rough fallacy*, for it is an informal fallacy with a very broad application. Could the ill-formatted and ketchup-stained sheaf of pages be the next great American novel? If we do not lock up this young man for home invasion, will he perhaps cure cancer? Is this typo-riddled resume perhaps the work of a misunderstood genius? In all these cases, we are faced with a clear indicator that something is bad, but the diamond in the rough fallacy would have us ignore those signs for fear that the thing might be good after all. And to exacerbate this propensity for second guessing ourselves, a sort of urban legend has sprung up around diamonds in the rough, about the genius who failed high school, or the salesman who turned away a man in shabby clothes only to discover the man was a millionaire.

Should we therefore read everything, just in case it is good? No, and for two reasons. First, it is impossible to read everything. There is too much published in philosophy in a single year for anyone to read it all. You would have to narrow your interests to one particular area of philosophy to even be able to read all that was written about it. But then you would be reading philosophy, not because of friendship with wisdom, but to achieve a complete overview of an area. That is hardly a very philosophical approach.

But the diamond in the rough fallacy is also at odds with what Aristotle (384 – 322 BC) called practical reason. In order to get our work done, we need to make general assumptions. A firm that interviewed or perhaps even hired those with lousy resumes just in case would waste more on interviewing and correcting than it stands to gain by finding a diamond. It is only those who have too much time on their hands who want to go searching for diamonds in the rough. The threescore years and ten of a man's life are not so very long. That is why there is no time for bad books.

As a practical matter, then, when a book is badly written, bloviating, wandering, it is not worth reading. In the same way that a bad resume is an indicator of someone who will not be good at work, a badly written book or article is an indicator of a muddled thinker. It isn't an infallible rule, but you will rarely be sorry you followed it.

6 - HOW TO FIND PHILOSOPHICAL COMMUNITY

WHY PHILOSOPHERS NEED OTHER PEOPLE

THE SOLITARY PHILOSOPHER

Philosophy, as we have seen, is friendship with wisdom. But wisdom is not a person, and friendship with wisdom is friendship in which only one person is involved, a solitary activity. The trouble is that while philosophy is inherently solitary, solitude does not agree with human beings. We are social animals; Aristotle (384 – 322 BC) thought that someone who lived outside of society must be either a beast or a god. I think he meant that for most of us, the framing conditions that allow us to work, live, and even to befriend wisdom, are social. Remove those framing conditions and our lives dissolve into an inward focused, animal existence. Those who could avoid becoming beasts must have been something more than human.

Ordinary people need other people, that is why even solitary collection hobbies have their own communities. If you collect stamps or guns or rare first editions, you long for the community of people who have the same interests. Philosophers are no different. We want to meet other philosophers, at least occasionally. We have collected ideas as carefully as anyone ever collected stamps, and we want to show them off. In this chapter, we look at ways in which you can find other philosophers.

There are three places to which solitary philosophers can go in search of community. You can hang around the university. You can try to convert colleagues at work or your loved ones to the philosophical cause. And you can figure out how to create new philosophical communities. You don't have to choose just one of these, of course. We will consider all three in this chapter.

THE UNIVERSITY

UNDERSTANDING THE INSTITUTION

The most important thing you need to know about the university today is that it is moving through a process of change toward an unknown destination. Perhaps the final state is one of complex entanglement with big business, or perhaps the university will become an extension of high school. Perhaps it will fail and collapse. It will help you, the solitary philosopher, to understand this transformation.

Universities formed about a thousand years ago. They took on the shape of other institutions of organized labour: the guild. Craftsmen and tradesmen in cities had banded together to ensure that anyone calling himself, say, a stonemason, would have a basic level of expertise. Every stonemason had to be a member of the stonemason's guild, which would apprentice him with a master until he gained the working rank, or degree, of journeyman. Further supervised work would allow him, if he chose, to try to become a master within the guild. If he succeeded then he too could raise up new guild members. From the point of view of the members, the guild functioned as a union: it demanded fair pay and good treatment of its members and did not allow non-members to compete in the trades. Members were made visible by a uniform that only they were allowed to wear. From the point of view of the rest of the city, the guild guaranteed service standards.

Scholars too founded guilds, which is why universities award degrees. Like stonemasons, scholars aimed to preserve the craft and ensure that new members were properly taught. Undergraduate students have no degree, which means they have no standing in the guild. The Bachelor's degree is the journeyman's degree, intended as a working level. The degree of Master (MA: Master of Arts) was at one time the last available degree in the university guild. But over time, additional degrees were added, including the doctorate and later, in Germany, the habilitation. The guild uniform was the academic gown, and senior guild members were marked by colorful hoods representing the degrees they held and where they had studied. The first universities were focused on a small core of subjects: theology, medicine, law and later, philosophy. That is why there are medical doctors (MDs), doctors of theology (DDs, Doctors of Divinity), and lawyers (JDs, the letters stand for *Juris Doctor*). Because it arrived last, the PhD (*Philosophiae Doctor*, in English, Doctor of Philosophy) eventually came to include many then non-existent arts. If you get your doctorate in geography, English, or anthropology, you receive a PhD.

For most of their history, universities were small institutions with which only perhaps five percent of the population were involved. Students who were poor but clever attended on scholarships; the children of the wealthy came to pick up some culture and receive what was called the gentleman's C. But over the course of the 20th century universities began to expand, driven by ideologies of equality. Didn't everyone deserve the chance to study important questions? Three quarters of a century later, the expansion and its consequences continue. One consequence of expansion was that standards had to fall, and they did. Another consequence, this one less predictable, was that as universities got bigger they became more and more like other businesses, with the same managerial structure. Where previously senior professors had been in charge, administration now tends to be put in the hands of professional administrators, often with little academic understanding but outranking even senior professors.

The future of the institution is uncertain, because the university really sells one luxury item: a credential. Luxury items have value when other people do not have one and cannot easily get one. Degrees used to be like Rolexes: getting a degree was difficult and they were only for sale in a few places. Nowadays degrees are to be had easily and everywhere; student bodies continue to expand and standards continue to fall, and yet the university continues to operate as a luxury retailer and the price of tuition goes up. Eventually, it seems, this bubble must burst.

For the solitary philosopher, all of this matters only as background information when considering how best to interact with the university. The parts of the university that will be most receptive to you will be the remnants of the old guild: professors, their talks and conferences and reading groups.

MAKING CONTACT WITH PROFESSORS

One of the open secrets of professional philosophy is that, if you allow your name to appear on the internet in any capacity associated with professional philosophy, you will be contacted by people from all around the world, and many of these people will be crazy. They will send you their secret formula which resolves all the mysteries of physics, or their three-step plan for world peace. When you get in touch with a professor, your first challenge is to distinguish yourself from these people.

Fortunately, there is a very simple way to strike up a conversation with a philosopher and to persuade him that you are not crazy. Read his books, or his articles, read *something* that he has written. Consider what he has said and ask him a meaningful question that shows you have read it and thought about it. You can ask for clarification or elaboration or even raise an objection that seems to you to be unanswered. Everyone likes to talk about his own work. If you are getting in touch with a professional philosopher, you probably want to talk about his work too, so open with that. You might think this is obvious, but hardly anyone ever does it.

You can also visit professors in person during office hours. Many professors have an office and are obliged to post and keep certain hours when they will be available to students. In North America, semesters run September to December, and January to April. At the end of each semester the office will be full of students trying to cry their way to an A, but early on the professor is likely to be all alone. That's when you can drop by and introduce yourself.

TALKS AND CONFERENCES

As a solitary philosopher, you can also benefit from talks and conferences held at the university. There is often much to be learned from the speakers, and such venues can help you to meet other philosophers.

Talks are one-off events, usually hosted by a philosophy department, where an invited expert presents his research and answers questions afterward. Every department of philosophy tries to host several talks every semester. The speaker wants to address a full room, and it is embarrassing for a university to invite a speaker and then not be able to provide an audience, so you will not be unwelcome. Just show up and take a seat.

Conferences are gatherings of experts, each presenting research loosely clustered around a theme (you can expect to see some papers linked to it very loosely indeed). A conference can last one day or several and will have a fixed schedule with time for questions allotted for each presentation. Sometimes after a paper another philosopher will have prepared comments, meaning that he will briefly summarize the presentation and raise a few questions for discussion.

In the English-speaking world, you can expect a lively question period after talks and conferences. The product that the speaker has presented is tested by his fellow philosophers, and sometimes you will see speakers stumped and unable to reply. You will learn a lot by listening to other people ask questions, watching these expert product testers react to a new product. You can ask questions too, of course: for clarification, for further comment, or you can raise an objection if you think the argument does not work.

There is no single way to find out what talks or conferences are happening near you. If you go looking on the internet, areas of philosophy (ancient philosophy, say, or philosophy of science) will often have their own websites devoted to upcoming conferences. Otherwise word is distributed through email lists, websites, and the home pages of departments of philosophy.

If your goal is to get to know people, it is best to stay for the whole conference, ask good questions, and perhaps hang around and see whether you can get invited to lunch or dinner. Some talks and conferences require you to pay to attend. When you are looking for a chance to talk to academic philosophers, small talks and conferences are better than big ones, and free ones are better than paid ones. That is because at a small event you are more likely to meet elements of your local philosophy scene. You are also less likely to encounter professors who are only there to advance their careers.

Once you have gotten the hang of conferences, you can send in a submission of your own. Conferences are announced with a call for papers. The organizers are inviting people to send in either a fully written presentation or, in some cases, an abstract: a punchy paragraph explaining what you are going to say. They will evaluate what comes in and tell you if you are accepted. If you have a paper or an idea for a paper, you can submit it. In your submission you should identify yourself as an 'independent scholar', which is the term for a scholar who is not currently affiliated with any university. It can be competitive. Even experienced presenters are often rejected. If your submission isn't accepted don't be discouraged, just keep trying.

TREATING THE UNIVERSITY AS A RESOURCE

Some philosophers who are not professional philosophers go to great lengths to become part of the conference circuit, publish in academic journals, and otherwise fit themselves into the university system. This requires overcoming some suspicion and even mild hostility, though probably not much more than an outsider would encounter on the way into any other industry. If you are considering pushing your way into the university as an outsider, though, I encourage you to ask yourself why. The only good reason I can think of is that you have niche interests. If you want to specialize in 19th century Russian philosophy, say, or in Ludwig Wittgenstein (1889 – 1951) interpretation, then probably the only people who will know as much as you do about your topic are professors, so you will have to hang around with them. But if your goal is merely to receive a pat on the head from the 'real philosophers' then I have written this book to dissuade you.

For all but a tiny fraction of people with very narrow interests, it is much easier to treat the university as a resource. You've already paid for it with your taxes, after all. Professional philosophers can help with obscure questions. If you are interested in a particular conference or a particular talk, show up and ask your questions, but don't feel obliged to stay for the whole thing unless you want to make friends. Academic libraries typically offer library cards for a price. This may be worthwhile, but nowadays books are cheap and most philosophy is available on the internet.

ACADEMIC DEAD ENDS

Even in its modern form, the university still contains much that is true, beautiful and good. When these things are available to you, make use of them. But there are also characteristic ways in which thinking in the university goes wrong, what I call academic dead ends. When you are dealing with the university you should be on your guard for these things.

Philosophical fashions. No single person ever decided that top hats, big hairdos, or bellbottom pants were no longer fashionable. Fashions are herd behaviours. Just as birds and fish can move together in large numbers, the human herd decides all at once that bellbottoms are no longer *in*. Probably every group generates in-group fashions, and academic philosophy is no exception.

In previous chapters, I spoke about the mysteriously long shadow of Immanuel Kant (1724 – 1804) which fell over the last two centuries of philosophy. This did not happen because Kant's arguments were so compelling. It was rather a philosophical fashion that emerged over the same period and for the same inscrutable reasons as the necktie. Another example: until the early 1980s, discussions in ethics were dominated by the ethics of duty and the ethics of consequence, but the publication in 1981 of *After Virtue* by Alasdair MacIntyre (b. 1929) reintroduced the ancient ethics of virtue, which soon became as fashionable as it had been unfashionable before. Once you get to know a specific department of philosophy, you will find that fashions exist within it. I studied in one department that was wild about evolutionary explanations, and another where the history of philosophy was always held to be crucial for understanding the present.

Fashions are not in themselves bad, and they do not necessarily lead to bad philosophy. For example, the return to virtue ethics greatly improved that branch on the tree of knowledge, and I think that the history of philosophy *really is* important if you want to understand the present. But we should believe things for good reasons, and the fact that something is fashionable is not a good reason for believing it. If you follow fashion you have no guarantee that you are following where wisdom leads. The closer you are to the academy, the more insistently these fashions will tug at you. As an outsider, though, you have the chance to visit the academy while still treating it as a strange land with customs and fashions that are not your own.

Triviality. Another academic dead end is triviality. Triviality is the consequence of the university's openness to questions that no one else is asking, its universality. Because the university will not guide what professors study, it sometimes happens that they choose things that are not worth studying. The university would allow you, for example, to spend your life working on a minor philosopher like Xenophon (430 – 354 BC), someone who does not really have a great deal to say. Now of course Xenophon is worth reading once, and in particular his recollections of his teacher Socrates (469 – 399 BC) are valuable. But a life spent reading Xenophon would be a life poorly spent.

Toilers in triviality may provide a valuable service to the rest of us. Their lifetime of work can produce the summary you need to understand a vexing question. Indeed, such professors may be able to help you with very specialized questions you encounter in your own studies. The trick is to benefit from the work of those who have descended into triviality without being drawn into it yourself.

Political correctness. Professors view themselves as standing apart from society, truth speakers unbent by the winds of contemporary doctrine. This is mostly wishful thinking. When ordinary working people encounter political correctness, they must accommodate it to a stubbornly resistant real world. Professors, on the other hand, encounter politically correct ideas as concepts without tangible consequences. For this reason, I think, universities have always been blown this way and that by politics.

In the minds of those vulnerable to it, political correctness usually trumps philosophical argument. This makes it a philosophical dead end. Soviet philosophers denounced great philosophers for being bourgeois. In the same way, many philosophers today waste time condemning the great philosophers for political sins that are meaningless outside our historical moment, or they insist on reading worse philosophers because they resent the fact that the great philosophers are mostly white males. Unlike philosophical fashion and triviality, which can at least lead to something good, political correctness is a dead end without any redeeming features.

Sooner rather than later, when you attend talks and conferences or when you speak to professors you will encounter these dead ends. To some extent these things have always been present, but today many professors fear the wrath of their politically correct colleagues and try to take refuge in triviality or in philosophical fashions in an effort to avoid controversy. If you were setting out to save the university, this would be something to worry about. If you were thinking about sending a son or daughter into the university, its current state should make you think again. But for those of us merely wanting to pass through it, an ironic smile is a good response to anyone trying to lead you down some philosophical dead end.

PHILOSOPHY, WORK, AND LOVE

THE PHILOSOPHER AT WORK

Since many who are introduced to philosophy do not become professors, they usually need to learn (or relearn) the lesson that philosophy is like stamp or gun collecting: it is an interest that most people will not share. Some philosophers resist this lesson and try to make converts for philosophy at work. But as they learn to their disappointment, a desire for friendship

6 - How to Find Philosophical Community

with wisdom does not lie dormant in every heart. If you try to turn your colleagues into philosophers, you will be as obnoxious as the fellow who keeps trying to tell you about his grandchildren or his vacations.

Although overt philosophy does not mix well with work, being a philosopher will make you better at almost anything in the white-collar world, and it will help with the administrative side of any practical work. Philosophy allows you to visualize a problem, seeing its abstract shape and anticipating points of weakness. It will let you summarize problems so that other people can see them almost as clearly as you do. Unfortunately, even the prospect of acquiring this skill will not tempt your colleagues to become philosophers, because in order to get it you need to take an interest in the parts of philosophy that have nothing to do with work. It would be like trying to convince someone who would like to be able to jog up a few stairs to his home that he could do it if only he ran a marathon. You are unlikely, therefore, to find a philosophical community at work.

It does not follow, though, that philosophy has no place at work. For one thing, work is a rich subject of philosophical inquiry. Since most professors do not have much experience of a 9 to 5 job, surprisingly little has been said or thought about work from a philosophical perspective.

Philosophy, Work, and Love | 207

Philosophy can also orient you at work. It can be an anchor to help you not to be swept away by office politics and the fads of management 'science'. But it can also be an escape, the quiet space in your mind where you can take stock of things, what Michel de Montaigne (1533 – 1592) described as the room behind the shop. For example, the best way I have found to endure a tedious meeting is to bring a notebook and a philosophical puzzle to work through step by step until it is clear in my mind.

THE PHILOSOPHER AT HOME

Just as some philosophers try to fit their interests into their working lives, others try to build romantic relationships with philosophy in the centre. It can work. Peter Geach (1916 – 2013) and Elizabeth Anscombe (1919 – 2001) were an exemplary philosophical couple. But most philosophers marry non-philosophers, and I think that may be for the best.

Socrates (469 – 399 BC) seems to have been married several times, but when one mentions Socrates' wife, most people think of Xanthippe (born 5th century BC). She was a woman who famously had no time for philosophy. She once interrupted Socrates' conversation outside their house in Athens by shouting at him from a window and finally, when he did not listen, emptying a chamber pot onto his head.

"After the thunder," remarked Socrates, not particularly concerned, "comes the rain."

Socrates and Xanthippe are a trope: the unworldly philosopher and his worldly wife. Xanthippe can't see beyond the empty pantry; Socrates misses the empty pantry for the stars. For some reason, readers have always taken sides. Some condemn Xanthippe for dragging the great man down to earth. Feminists make Xanthippe a symbol of their grievances. It seems to me that both sides miss the obvious. Socrates – or Xanthippe – could have sought a divorce. In fact Socrates never spoke badly of his wife, indeed he said that he liked that she had a mind of her own. Xenophon (430 – 354 BC) records a conversation where Socrates uses his famous Socratic method of question and answer to explain to his angry son just how much his mother loved him. The evidence suggests that Socrates and Xanthippe were happy. In Socrates and Xanthippe, I see two complementary forces; a dramatization of the conflict between the sexes which forms a greater whole. The father of philosophy was a great man, and history presents him to us paired with a woman able to keep him anchored to the world. That is why, of his two marriages, it is the one with Xanthippe that we remember.

A NEW SOCIETY WITHIN THE SHELL OF THE OLD

AS THE UNIVERSITY FAILS

Although you should take what you can from the university, unless you enter it as a student or professor, it is not likely to offer you a place. Even if you did become a permanent member, you would find philosophy in revolt against its own history. I have also suggested that it is fruitless to seek philosophical community at work, and unwise to create it in one's home life. Where, then, is the philosopher to go?

Plato's (429 – 347 BC) *Symposium* describes a philosophy party held by the friends of Socrates (369 – 399 BC). They like to hang around together; one night they decide not to get drunk but instead to go around the room with each man giving his thoughts on the nature of love. What emerges is not academic. It's better than that. The answers are literary, comic, and philosophical. The formula is simple: a group of thoughtful friends willing to talk.

Again and again over the course of the history of philosophy, philosophers find themselves in the position of the friends of Socrates: meeting in homes without any institutional connection whatsoever. But there is one period that is a model for our own: the so-called Early Modern period, running roughly 1600 –

1800. The period was shaped by challenges like the ones that face us today.

By the end of the middle ages and into the Renaissance, the university was dominant, but its methods were hardening and becoming inward-focused. In order to become a master, a student had to memorize a vast array of argument structures, get used to nitpicking distinctions, master the baroque metaphysical terminology that had grown out of Aristotle, and grow familiar with the many, many masters who had proceeded him. The result was philosophy that is almost unreadable today. Even though there is so much pressure to dig up historical material and write about it, few can be bothered to dig up the needlessly complex writings of the Early Modern university. As the middle ages came to an end, philosophers looking in were disgusted by the formulas and the jargon and the sheer boringness of the academy. The university was no place for a friend of wisdom. And so, philosophy began to bloom elsewhere.

When we remember the 17th and 18th centuries, we remember philosophers operating outside of institutions: René Descartes (1596 – 1650), G. W. Leibniz (1646 – 1716), Baruch Spinoza (1632 – 1677), Denis Diderot (1713 – 1784), Voltaire (1694 – 1778), Jean Jacques Rousseau (1712 – 1778), John Locke (1632 – 1704), George Berkeley (1685 –1753), for most of his life) and David Hume (1711 – 1776). Some intelligent young people still attended university, though not all did so. Very few of them wanted to have anything to do with the place after they graduated. We retroactively recognize that the philosophers who mattered were the ones who saw what had happened to the university and chose to make their philosophical homes outside it, in clubs and salons or through correspondence networks.

Our situation is like that of those philosophers in the 17th and 18th centuries. Universities are becoming bogged down both by how they think and by what they think about. The academic publishing system makes it difficult to write beautifully and well. And whether through personal cowardice or genuine belief, many professional philosophers are more interested in condemning the great philosophers of the past than in reading them. The situation was similarly bleak at the end of the middle ages. And the solution is similar too: those of us interested in philosophy should build philosophical community elsewhere.

If that seems daunting, we need to remember three things. First, although the university is an alliance of disciplines, a brotherhood of scholars, outside the university we are all on our own. We philosophers must save philosophy, and any alliance with other scholars, with sociologists, geographers, biologists, or physicists should be maintained only if it helps the cause of philosophy. Such an alliance might have value, but we can and should be discerning. If philosophers can make common cause with physicists and biologists, it does not follow that we should care whether communications or English or leisure studies vanish from the earth.

There is a second way in which the task is more manageable than it might at first seem. We do not need to recreate the institutional structure of the university, either its teaching or administrative structure. What is good about it can be appropriated, the rest does not matter. We might take encouragement from the observation of the International Workers of the World (the "Wobblies") in another context, who talked about "forming the structure of the new society within the shell of the old." The Wobblies' insight is that there is never a single moment of transformation. The old institutions will not vanish; no one will hand you the keys to the future and say that from here on out it is up to you. Yes, the university is fading into irrelevance. But its structure will still be there for some time. Use it, but do not rely on it. With that in mind what you need to do is form a local, perhaps temporary home, a place where you can try out ideas, but also a base from which to launch forays into the crumbling architecture and rewilding lands of academia.

The third thing we need to remember is that the formula for a philosophical group is simple. All that is needed is a few motivated philosophers: Plato's circle of smart friends willing to put off a raucous party to spend the night sipping wine and trying to understand the nature of love. And even this simple formula is worked out in several different ways in the period that will be our guide, the early modern period.

THE REPUBLIC OF LETTERS

The internet offers abundant opportunities for building philosophical societies. It is easy to set up a blog, or to comment on someone else's blog. It's easy, also, to get in touch with people anywhere in the world.

In some ways, the internet is our equivalent to the letter-writing networks that existed in the 17th and 18th centuries, and which went by several beautiful names, including "the Republic of Letters" and "the Invisible College". Through this network, philosophers and other scholars who were spread throughout the regions of Europe and North America were able to test one another's ideas.

The Republic of Letters had one important advantage over the state of philosophy on the internet, and this is that the Republic of Letters was shaped around individuals who acted as hubs, connecting readers and writers. This controlled the quality of what was went through the network.

The internet has brought the cost of engagement far down, and now anyone with access to a computer can read and write philosophy. The task of moderating all these contributions would exhaust any gatekeeper. As a result, philosophy on the internet tends to be locally moderated in blogs and magazines and unmoderated overall. This is a problem, but it could also be an opportunity. There is room on the internet for blogs devoted to a traditional approach to the great philosophers of the past. More hubs and more gatekeepers are needed.

The internet also makes possible networks that have many of the advantages of dialogue. Podcasts are an example of this. Readers with a specific interest can read and come together to discuss a particular work of philosophy in such a way that others can benefit from their discussion. Even the podcasters do not have to be in the same place. The comments section for the podcast, if there is one, can become a hub, and the podcasters can function as gatekeepers.

CLUBS

Alongside the Republic of Letters, non-academic philosophers of the 17th and 18th centuries met in person in clubs and salons. They met to discuss new ideas, consider one another's writing and research, and to hear visitors. Since philosophers in this period were not trying to meet any sort of departmental standard for publishing, they read widely, wrote rarely, and produced works that do not fit easily into the way we categorize knowledge today. They wrote on what we would call physics, psychology, history, and philology, as well as in more traditional areas of philosophy.

Many groups of this sort already exist. Philosophy departments sometimes form reading groups, populated largely with graduate students. Some of these have themes (the philosophy of religion, say) and others are attached to courses. For example, a professor teaching a course on medieval philosophy might pair it with an optional reading group focusing on a particular medieval text, perhaps to be read in Latin. If you scout the websites of philosophy departments, you'll get wind of these sorts of groups.

Universities are also orbited by more formal clubs where members and visitors present their work. These are often based on a topic (say, the philosophy of science) or a period (say, the 18th century). At their nicest, these are elegant meetings which begin with conversation over drinks and feature engaging speakers and lively questions afterward.

Casting the net wider still, bookstores and libraries often encourage the formation of reading groups, since these are likely to use their wares. You can also find reading groups associated with political movements and churches.

Beyond these, there are private clubs for gentlemen scholars to enjoy community and read and discuss books, or sometimes, read one another's work. You'll need to go looking for these, since they usually do not advertise.

FOUNDING A GROUP

If you can't find a philosophy group, then you may have to start one. Fortunately, this is not as difficult as you might imagine. You don't need very many people to have an enjoyable discussion about philosophy. Two or three is enough for a very satisfying product testing of one another's ideas. If you don't know two people with similar interests, then you might consider putting up a poster in a library or another community space, or seeking readers at your church.

Once you go looking for people, you will likely find that some of those who are drawn to your group are just lonely and have little real interest in the material. In my groups, I try to tolerate such people provided they do not actively steer the conversation away from philosophical questions. It seems to me that they may learn something, even it if is only how to ask clarifying questions. But you will need at least one other person who is able and willing to talk about the material, or else the group will have no purpose.

For a location, you will need a place that is reasonably quiet. You can invite people to meet in your home if you know them well enough. A pub will do, if the music isn't too loud. Alcohol acts as a social lubricant, and for many people the relaxation of mind brought about by moderate drinking can make them more open-minded in discussion – that's the plot of Plato's *Symposium*, after all. Otherwise there are cafés and restaurants. I was once part of a very successful group that met in the morning before work in a greasy spoon café.

If you founded the group, it's your group. So you will need to consider some questions to get you started:

What is your group's goal? The goal of a philosophical group is, of course, to pursue friendship with wisdom. But it helps to have a secondary goal in mind. Perhaps you want to work your way through the great history of philosophy. Perhaps you want to examine a particular branch of the tree of knowledge. Perhaps you want to explore a particular question. Or perhaps you would like to discuss your own writing and that of other participants. Any of these are good goals. Choosing one will help answer some of the other questions.

If you're not sure where to start, I have included a list of some books of great philosophers after this chapter. I've indicated their topics, and also marked some that will be of special interest to beginners.

How much can your group read between meetings? Most book clubs read one book every month, and that book becomes the topic of discussion for the group. Unless the book is supremely bad, reading it ahead of time pretty much guarantees there will be plenty to talk about. One of the questions you'll have to ask yourself is how much people are willing to read. There are a couple of things that might make you consider shortening the reading requirements. First, some philosophical readings are dense. For example, Plato's *Republic* is made up of ten chapters. There is so much in each of the chapters that a philosophy group could easily go chapter by chapter and still have plenty to discuss. Second, members of your group may be too busy (or they may think they are too busy) to read a full book. Perhaps a chapter or an article that they can think about while they work would be better. But don't be too quick to react to complaints of busyness. People who constantly complain about the length of the readings are probably not very interested in philosophy.

How will you get the texts? You can find pretty much all the books of great philosophers online, in good translations, and for free, especially if you are creative about it. Academic books are absurdly expensive and generally not worth the money. But most of the books that matter can be had fairly cheaply in a used copy. Even so, it is worth asking yourself the logistical question of how people are going to get the readings.

Does membership in your reading group impose a cost on each member, every month, to buy a book? Will they have to find the book online themselves? Or will you circulate a PDF version of the reading in advance? And if you do that, will readers print everything, or put things on a phone, or on a tablet... or what? If you are going to read one another's work, how soon before the meeting must the work be circulated, and how? In my experience, mobile phones are too distracting and tiny for anyone to read from. Tablets are generally fine.

Will there be a summary at the beginning? One way to keep a reading group on track is to have someone take on the role of summarizing the reading, and then begin each meeting with a summary of the text. The summary should be short, no longer than five minutes. The summarizer concludes with a few questions or observations about the text, something to start conversation if no one can think of anything to say. The summarizer refreshes the memories of the other participants to ensure that the reading is clear in their minds. He should have a few interesting points prepared, but the choices he makes in his summary may prompt discussion on their own. And, most crucially, the summarizer will represent the text as an ambassador, trying to defend it if everyone else thinks it is bad.

Why bother with this ritual? Well, the summarizer provides a service to the group. He may find he has to argue against everybody and give a defence of the text, even if that defence is conditional or qualified. In this way, the role of the summarizer is to exemplify the historian's virtue of charity, the rule by which we apply the best possible interpretation to the writings of the great philosophers. He brings the text to life, and deflects objections raised against it whenever he can. This makes the meeting more interesting for everybody else.

The real beneficiary, though, will be the summarizer himself. By taking ownership of a position in philosophy he will be forced to use his philosophical compass. When someone critiques the text, the summarizer will need to search the philosophical map to find a way to defend against that criticism. What is more, when reading great books of philosophy, the summarizer is taking on the ideas of a philosophical giant. Even if he is not persuaded, he will catch a glimpse of the world through the eyes of a truly great philosopher. Very often the summarizer walks away with a better understanding than anyone else. The experience of summarizing is in this way like teaching, for only by taking responsibility for a text can one really understand it.

The role of summarizer is valuable, so I suggest that it rotates between members of the group. The nature of that rotation will be decided depending on...

Who is going to be in charge? You might suppose that reading groups would function best on a democratic model, but it is not so. For one thing, someone will have to decide on the reading group's goal, and on what exactly will be read. To some extent, this can be decided democratically, provided that you have rules, but then someone will have to set those rules. For example, the group as a whole might decide on the next reading. Or the choice might cycle around through group members. In my experience, groups are usually stabilized by one or a few strong personalities. If you are the founder, the person in charge is likely to be you. It will fall to the *de facto* leader to resolve questions like...

What will you do about people who don't read the book? You will eventually encounter the problem of people who don't do the reading but want to come to the discussion anyway, and people whose contribution is never any good. If no one does the readings, then perhaps you need to make them shorter. If one person is never prepared and everyone else's time is being wasted explaining the reading to him, perhaps eventually he will need to go. One useful rule is that if you haven't done the reading, you cannot partake in the discussion, you become a listening member, and you get no vote in what will be read next. Shame works.

Who will keep things on track? Philosophy groups tend to turn into social groups. Members will want to catch up on one another's news, they will become friends. This is all to the good, but if you want the group to have philosophical value, you will need to carve out a portion of the time you spend together that really is for philosophy and nothing else. For example, you might say that there will be an hour of discussion of the text. If people want to catch up before or after the hour, that's fine, so long as it doesn't cut into the hour. During the hour, your task will be to police the conversation and not let it wander away from philosophy.

WHAT THERE IS TO BE DONE

Starting a podcast or a blog or a reading or discussion group may seem a little underwhelming. Even if you agree that the university has lost its way, one little a group may not seem much of a dissident alternative. But although groups start small, they can grow. Groups that endure can become cultural institutions in their own right. They can become venues for visiting speakers. They can even be sources for new ventures. One reading group that I used to attend grew into a liberal arts college.

Your group can also be a base from which you carry out other activities. Someone needs to organize philosophical hubs on the internet. Someone needs to publish magazines of traditional philosophy, and then many others need to fill these magazines with articles. Someone needs to offer alternative pathways into philosophy, for example to homeschoolers. Someone needs to bring Christian philosophy to churches.

As universities increasingly refuse to teach or even preserve books by the great philosophers, there will be lessons to offer and texts to preserve. Great books need to be preserved in digital copies, but also republished without fashionable, politically correct or trivial commentary. As universities become ever more pedantic, there will be work to be done bridging the divide of disciplines, perhaps reading together with those of other backgrounds to make philosopher-scientists and scientific philosophers. As the liberal world order gives way to something new, fearless philosophers will need to understand the political reordering that must follow.

These are the problems like those that philosophers of the 17th and 18th century solved from within their small groups. So if you are worried that there is little you can do as a solitary philosopher, then put your mind at ease. There is plenty to be done.

THE FIRST STEP

The very first step is to begin a friendship with wisdom. We must take this first step, for wisdom does not need us, it is we who need her. Wisdom is a constant friend, but she will not seek us out.

There is a story about a man who goes to an old European art gallery. He passes quickly through, unimpressed by the old masters on display. On the way out, he tells the curator that he saw nothing that he liked.

"Aha, no," replies the curator, "you have misunderstood. These paintings are no longer on trial. The visitor is on trial."

Before the great philosophers of the past, before wisdom herself, we would-be philosophers are on trial, along with the times and places that we live in. Many people fail this trial. Entire times and places fail as well, and consequently do not even rate a mention in the history of philosophy. Will we do better? That is up to us.

A PHILOSOPHY READING LIST

Below you will find a list of books by, or in some cases about, the great philosophers. The readings are in rough historical order. To keep the list relatively short, I have limited it to books.

I have listed authors and titles only because, with a few exceptions, it doesn't matter what editions you get. One of the exceptions are fragments: it is hard to find good editions and I have listed some of the better ones. The other exceptions to look out for are abridged and 'simplified' texts. Whether you want to read an abridged version is up to you, and some works do benefit from being abridged. For example, even John Locke thought his *Essay Concerning Human Understanding* could do with a trim. But I'd usually rather be the judge of what is and what is not worth reading. Simplified texts are translated from older

English into modern English. As a rule, the older texts are worth the trouble, and simplified texts are not very good.

Fragments of the Presocratics. A couple of good collections are:

> G. S. Kirk, J. E. Raven and M. Schofield, *The Presocratic Philosophers* (Cambridge: Cambridge University Press, 1983)

> Robin Waterfield, *The First Philosophers: the Presocratics and the Sophists* (Oxford: Oxford University Press, 2000)

Plato: *Euthyphro** [**M**], *Apology** [**M**, **Eth**], *Crito* [**Eth**], *Phaedo* [**M**], *Gorgias* [**Eth**], *Symposium* [**M**], *Republic** [**M**, **Ep**, **Eth**]

Fragments of Diogenes the Cynic

> A good collection is: Robin Hard, *Diogenes the Cynic, Sayings and Anecdotes: With Other Popular Moralists* (Oxford: Oxford World Classics, 2012)

Aristotle: *Nicomachean Ethics** [**M**, **Eth**], *Physics** [**M**], *De Anima* [**M**], *Metaphysics** [**M**]

Fragments of the Hellenistic Philosophers. A couple of good collections are:

> Brad Inwood and Lloyd P. Gerson, *Hellenistic Philosophy: Introductory Readings* (Indianapolis: Hackett, 1988/1997)

> A. A. Long and David Sedley, *The Hellenistic Philosophers* (Cambridge: Cambridge University Press, 1987), 2 vols. **Note:** the second volume contains the Greek and Latin fragments, it's worth the money if you have the languages, otherwise just buy volume 1.

Marcus Tullius Cicero: *On the Nature of the Gods** [**M, Th**]

Lucius Anneus Seneca (a.k.a. Seneca the Younger): *On the Happy Life* [**Eth**]

Titus Lucretius Carus: *On the Nature of Things* (a.k.a. *De Rerum Natura*) [**M, Eth, Th**]

Epictetus: *Handbook** (a.k.a. *Guide, Encheiridion*) [**Eth, M**]

Marcus Aurelius Antoninus Augustus: *Meditations* (a.k.a. *The Emperor's Handbook*) [**Eth, M**]

Plotinus: *Enneads* [**M**]

St. Augustine of Hippo: *Confessions** [**Eth**, **Th**, **M**]

Anicius Manlius Severinus Boethius: *Consolation of Philosophy** [**Eth**]

St. Anselm of Canterbury: *Proslogion** [**M**, **Th**]

St. Thomas Aquinas: *Summa Theologica** (a.k.a. *Summa Theologiae*) [**Th**, **M**, **Eth**, **Ep**, **Pol**], *Summa Contra Gentiles* [**Th**, **M**, **Eth**, **Ep**, **Pol**]. These are long books. I would recommend reading selections. Excellent selections arranged around different topics can be had from Hackett press, but you can also flip through the table of contents and use St. Thomas as a reference book.

Nicolo Machiavelli: *The Prince* [**Pol**]

Michel de Montaigne: *Essays* [**M**, **Eth**, **Ep**,]

René Descartes: *Meditations on First Philosophy** [**M**, **Ep**], *Discourse on the Method* [**M**, **Ep**, **Sci**]

Thomas Hobbes: *Leviathan* [**Pol**, **M**]

Nicolas Malebranche: *Search After Truth* [**M**, **Ep**]

Bernard Mandeville: *The Fable of the Bees* [**Ec**]

Baruch Spinoza: *Ethics* [**M**]

John Locke: *An Essay concerning Human Understanding* [**Ep, M**]

G. W. Leibniz: *Discourse on Metaphysics* [**M**], *Theodicy** [**Th, M**], *Monadology* [**M**]

George Berkeley: *Three Dialogues Between Hylas and Philonous** [**M, Ep**]

David Hume: *An Enquiry concerning Human Understanding** [**M, Ep**]

Thomas Reid, *Essays on the Intellectual Powers of Man* [**M, Ep**]

Adam Smith, *The Wealth of Nations* [**Ec**]

Immanuel Kant: *Prolegomena to any Future Metaphysics** [**M, Ep**], *Grounding of the Metaphysics of Morals* [**Eth**], *Critique of Pure Reason* [**M, Ep**]

Edmund Burke: *Reflections on the Revolution in France* [**Pol**]

Arthur Schopenhauer: *The World as Will and Representation* [**M, Ep**], Essays (any collection will have something interesting)

John Stuart Mill: *Utilitarianism** [**Eth**], *On Liberty** [**Pol**]

Karl Marx: *Das Kapital* [**Ec, Pol**], *The Communist Manifesto* (with Friederich Engels) [**Pol, Ec**]

Soren Kierkegaard: *Fear and Trembling* [**Eth**]

Friederich Nietzsche: *Thus Spake Zarathustra* [**Eth**]

G. K. Chesterton: *Orthodoxy** [**Eth, Th, M**]

Ludwig Wittgenstein: *Tractatus Logico-Philosophicus* [**L, Ep**], *Philosophical Investigations* [**L, Ep**]

Carl Schmitt: *The Concept of the Political* [**Pol**]

Martin Heidegger: *Being and Time* [**M**]

Eric Hoffer: *The True Believer** [**Pol**]

Willard van Orman Quine: *From a Logical Point of View** [**L, M, Ep**]

Russell Kirk: *The Conservative Mind* [**Pol**]

J. L. Austin: *How to do things with Words** [**L**]

John Rawls: *A Theory of Justice* [**Pol**]

Robert Nozick: *Anarchy, State and Utopia* [**Pol**]

Bernard Williams: *Moral Luck* [**M**, **Eth**]

Alasdair MacIntyre: *After Virtue** [**Eth**]

Ian Hacking: *Representing and Intervening: Introductory Topics in the Philosophy of Science** [**Sci**, **M**, **Ep**], *Why does Language Matter to Philosophers** [**L**, **M**]

Saul A. Kripke: *Wittgenstein on Rules and Private Language* [**L**]

David Stove: *The Plato Cult and Other Philosophical Follies* [**M**, **Ep**], *On Benevolence** [**Pol**]

John Gray: *Enlightement's Wake** [**Pol**]

Roger Scruton: *On Beauty** [**Aes**]

Thomas Nagel: *The View from Nowhere* [**Ep**, **M**], *Mind and Cosmos** [**M**]

GUIDE TO THE LIST

Asterisk (*): Readings marked with the asterisk will help to introduce you to philosophy, they are good for beginners. The reason is not that they are simpler (in may cases the opposite is true). It is rather that they are clear and comprehensive, which makes them like mountains from which you can get a good view of the surrounding philosophical countryside.

Ancient Names: Many ancient philosophers are remembered by only a portion of their names, which can be confusing to modern readers. The philosopher Marcus Tullius Cicero, for example, is known to us today as Cicero. I have given names in full but underlined the parts of their names that we use today.

Topics: One way to read through this list is by topic. I have added a letter after those titles which can easily be classified to indicate what the book is for the most part about. But beware, these are rough guides at best. Collections of fragments range over everything, and so I haven't marked them at all.

> **M** = Metaphysics
>
> **Ep** = Epistemology
>
> **Eth** = Ethics
>
> **Aes** = Aesthetics
>
> **Pol** = Politics
>
> **Sci** = Philosophy of science
>
> **Th** = Philosophical theology
>
> **Ec** = Philosophy of economics
>
> **L** = Philosophy of language

Made in the USA
Las Vegas, NV
08 February 2022

43401275R00134